FROM THE HEART
OF AN
INTERCESSOR

The Father's Heart Cry

Volume 1

David L. Thomas

ANderSON PublishiNG
DouglasvillE, GA

Anderson Publishing
P. O. Box 5544
Douglasville, GA 30154
www.andersonpub.com

CONTENTS

From The Heart of His Princess. . .a Tribute to Her Beloved Warrior

☞

As you read and pray the prayers found in this book, I challenge you to find on each page a love letter from my husband to the Body of Christ. These prayers are not merely written with ink, but with the all-powerful Spirit of the living God whom David loved and served fervently and passionately with all of his heart.

God unexpectedly whispered David's name on August 23, 2000 leaving so many of us without the one we loved to have pray for us and do spiritual battle for us. I am so honored to have been the one to be by his side all those years. He was the Job 29 man personified with a raging beauty and blazing holiness. I was blessed beyond measure by his example of tenacious, prevailing, and uncompromisingly righteous prayer. My years of spiritual "boot camp" at David's side are best described with Oswald Chamber's statement: *"prayer does not equip us for greater works, PRAYER IS THE GREATER WORK."*

The lifetime of hours he spent in the Father's throne room are recorded in Heaven. Now his life and testimony have been imparted to me and, with great resolve, I carry the mantle he left. I often hear his voice in my spirit as I pray and I hope that, as you turn the pages and read some of his mightiest prayers, you, too, will hear the voice of the one we all loved so dearly. Since the tragic events on September 11, 2001, I have asked that my two favorite prayers of his be included in this volume of prayers. They are entitled *Father Heal Our Land* and a *Prayer For Our Nation*. David knew many years earlier that America's only hope and security were for our nation to turn back to God.

It has been said that the unfinished friendships of this life suddenly become our dearest experiences and most glorious hopes. My beloved Warrior enriched my life with divine experiences that continue unto this day and will reach into eternity.

The words of Catherine of Sienna are forever etched in my testimony—"*Make two homes for thyself, my daughter. One actual home. . .and another spiritual home, which thou are to carry with thee always. . . .*" Although David died as we were building our actual new home together last year, the spiritual home he built for me was based on a firm foundation. It has not been diminished with his death but has grown and become a haven for others. Thank you, Warrior, for loving me with the heart of an intercessor, the very heart of God Himself. You are still my heartbeat and forever joined with us in the secret place of prayer.

~~*Princess*~~

FATHER HEAL OUR LAND

Dear Lord, raise up a company of worshippers in Atlanta who will lavishly praise You, and at this moment, help us to orchestrate together with a network of intercessors who can move in the awesome power of unified prayer.

Prepare our hearts, forgive our sins, cleanse us thoroughly by the blood of Jesus Christ so we can corporately pray effectual prayers which avail very, very much at this critical hour of our nation.

Lord, as our nation hangs in the balance, we are cast into the valley of decision, and time is of the essence. We pray that You would sovereignly move on Your people to take a resolute stand for righteousness, godliness, morality, and scriptural standards.

We pray that You would awaken a slumbering, complacent Church and with the stroke of Your hand, jolt us out of our apathy. Forgive us, Lord, for inhaling the deadly ether of the spirit of this age. We repent of allowing the enemy, as it states in the book of Joel, to overrun our walls and invade our homes while we were asleep. We repent on behalf of the Lord Jesus Christ in the last presidential election *[1996]*, that 40% of Christians didn't even trouble themselves enough to register to vote. Help them to realize what you say in Psalm 12:8,

**"The wicked freely strut about
when what is vile is honored among men."**

We repent of our lethargy which has allowed the same conditions to prevail as in the day of Isaiah which produced a dearth of heroes, warriors, judges, prophets, elders, captains, men of rank, counselors and skilled craftsmen.

We repent as the Church of the Lord Jesus Christ for allowing men in government who give safe haven and support to sodomites, perverts and the slaughter of the unborn. We repent as the Church for allowing those in government who will remove the Ten Commandments and prayer from school and support and encourage fornication by the dispensing of condoms. Etch into our brains and hearts the truth of Proverbs 14:34,

**"Righteousness exalts a nation,
but sin is a disgrace to any people."**

We repent of having become a nation of discards and rejects; our consciences have become cauterized, our hearts hardened and our sensitivities have become seared. Consequently, life has become cheap. We readily, without cringing, throw away babies just as if we were dispensing of bags, bottles and boxes. God, have mercy on us. The blood of these little ones is crying out to avenge such a holocaust in this nation. Move swiftly, Lord God Almighty, while Your hand is still extended, while we still are under Your grace.

Remove the evil stench which has flowed freely in our land ever since the brilliant "politically correct" amoral think tanks of the higher courts, who call light darkness and darkness light, have opened the floodgates for immoral putrefaction and raw sewage to flow freely in our schools, streets, and living rooms. In the place of this, bring back the wind of Your Spirit which is full of the fragrance and beauty of the Lord. Let God arise and the enemy be scattered. Bring back old-fashioned holiness and purity. Return to our society leadership who by their lives, influence, example and right decisions will restore integrity, moral values, and Godly ethics to this nation.

By Your grace, we will pay the price. We will be lovers of God more than lovers of pleasure. We will turn away from a creature-comfort mentality. We choose to leave the lap of luxury and the couch of comfort, trouble ourselves, and by the grace of God, we will become spiritual vigilantes. We pray according to Isaiah 62:1,

"For Zion's sake we will not keep silent, for Jerusalem's sake we will not remain quiet, till her righteousness shines out like the dawn, her salvation like a blazing torch."

We also pray according to that same passage that we would "awake, awake, put on our strength. . .; put on our beautiful garments, . . .shake ourselves from the dust; arise, sit erect in a dignified place, . . . and loose ourselves from the bonds of our neck . . ."

We pray to raise up the righteous and put down the wicked. Raise up men and women of God who don't have price tags hanging on them, who can't be bought at any price, who are not hypnotized by the smell of money. Raise up leaders who are more concerned about the moral climate of our country than they are of being re-elected. Bring forth men and women of God who can't be leveraged, manipulated, pressured, maneuvered, or controlled.

Bring a new generation of leaders who can move against the tide, who are not swept along by the spirit of this age, who are courageous, stalwart and have the spiritual fiber and moral fortitude to stand for righteousness; who honor the Godly foundation and roots of our nation and let the chips fall where they may. We plead for leaders who will boldly proclaim in the face of the gods, and the bad breath of the adversary himself, "As for me and my house, my administration, my office, my senate chambers, my jurisdiction of authority, we will serve the Lord!"

At this strategic hour of history, we plead with You, Lord God of Israel, to raise up Elijahs and Jeremiahs who will speak with a prophetically courageous voice and call this nation back to its moorings, back to its senses, back to its sanity, back to its foundation, back to its knees, and back to its God.

Lord, our children need to witness some Daniels, who in the face of dire pressure will throw open their blinds three times a day, get on their knees, and in the sight of the Asherahs, Baals' groves, images and peer pressure, declare that God is God above all gods, King above all kings, Lord of Lords, and witness the mouth of the lion being muzzled and shut by the angel of the Lord.

Lord, our children need to witness some Shadrachs, Meshachs and Abednegos who will not bend the knee to Baal, who will not capitulate to the pressures around them and rather will choose to be thrown into the fiery furnace, and be plucked out of the inferno without the smell of smoke by an astounded, trembling king who will freely acknowledge of a truth, Your God reigns.

Blow the trumpet in Zion; sound the alarm on Your holy hill. Give us Your grace, and a sense of urgency, we who are called by Your name to humble ourselves and pray and seek Your face, and turn from our wicked ways. Then, You will hear from heaven and will forgive our sin and will heal our land. Lord, Atlanta and America are hemorrhaging from perversion and wickedness. Our land desperately needs healing. We thank You that there is still time. Your grace is still extended over us. Your mercy is still evident. The window of opportunity is still open. Help us to buy up the time and apply our hearts to wisdom.

We ask You to raise up Godly fathers, Godly husbands, Godly councilmen, Godly mayors, governors, senators and a God-fearing president. We beseech You, Lord God Almighty, in Whom there is no shadow of turning, to raise up a Godly president, who does not have blood on His hands, to lead this nation. We place ourselves on an intercessory vigil. We move into a position of travailing prayer. We are willing to stand in the gap and make up the hedge, and be counted as one of Your prayer warriors.

We ask You, Lord, to raise up millions of green-beret prayer warrior intercessors who will storm the portals of heaven and plunder the gates of hell at one of the most crucial and pivotal times of the history of America. Rend the heavens, Lord, come down. Thank You for the promise, that when the enemy comes in like a flood, You will raise up a standard against him. We thank You also that when the enemy comes in, like a FLOOD You will raise up a standard against him.

We ask You, Lord, to bring a revival of intercessory prayer power to the extent, that once again we would be able to drive back the invading, dark hordes; put to flight the foreign alien armies of diabolical darkness; serve eviction papers on master spirits, territorial and world rulers, principalities, powers, spirit forces of wickedness, satanic highnesses and demonic nobilities. Reverse the trend. Create a vacuum of evil so righteousness can rule and reign. We thank You that according to scripture, when God arises, there is no contest. The only thing the enemy can do is to be thoroughly scattered.

By the grace and tenacity and resilience of the living God, we are going to pray 'til You raise up the righteous and put down the wicked and righteousness rules and reigns. We are going to pray 'til the environment of this city and our neighborhoods is not conducive for evil, but becomes a wellspring of righteousness, equity and morality. By the grace of God, we are going to pray 'til You put a halt to miscarriages of justice, and there will come forth from our court systems just and equitable decisions, and if those in authority refuse this kind of judicial integrity, You would replace them so speedily with Godly men and women, that it would cause heads to turn, ears to tingle, and send shock waves of the fear of God throughout Atlanta and this nation. Let the fear of God fall upon Atlanta and America. Lord, raise up in this nation stalwart, courageous Godly leadership that will act to silence the cry of blood that arises from the ground because of the carnage of over 30 million massacred babies, some of whom are future apostles, prophets, evangelists, teachers and pastors, that will be free of strange and perverse mixtures and will not embrace Sodom and Gomorrah, and at the same time spout off scripture out of context, who will contend for the widow and orphan and homeless, who will defend the righteous, who will have the spiritual authority to drive out from our school systems what scripture calls demonic desert beasts, screech owls, things that mutter and peep, and creep and crawl, and bring back the basics, reading, writing, 'rithmetic and righteousness.

Help us to pray until You raise up the righteous and put down the wicked until You would cause to ascend to Capitol Hill those spoken of in Psalm 24:3, 4 who have clean hands and a pure heart, who do not lift their soul to an idol or swear by what is false, who will receive a blessing from the Lord, and vindication from God their Savior, who will be part of the generation who seeks the Lord, who diligently seek the face of their God.

Etch graphically into our brains and hearts what Your Word says in Proverbs 14:34.

**"Righteousness exalts a nation,
but sin is a disgrace to any people."**

You are our rock and our fortress, for the sake of Your name lead and guide us (Psalm 31:3). Send forth Your light and Your truth, let them guide us, let them bring us to your holy mountain, to the place where you dwell (Psalm 43:3). From the ends of the earth we call to You, we call as our heart grows faint; lead us to the rock that is higher than us (Psalm 61:2). Lead us, Lord God, and raise up anointed, Godly leaders in this crucial hour.

Raise up the righteous, put down the wicked. Let God arise and the enemy be scattered. The victory is ours. The battle is the Lord's.

Thank You for hearing our prayer. We are greatly encouraged in the Lord this day. The effectual, fervent prayer of a righteous person avails very, very much.

In Jesus' name we pray. Amen.

PRAYER FOR OUR NATION

ୡ

Dear Lord, we declare today, in the power of corporate prayer, that the ruling spirit over Marietta and Cobb County is the Holy Spirit. Open the gates for the King of Glory to come in, the Lord strong and mighty, the Lord mighty in battle. Lord, we're hungry and thirsty and desperate for You. Our soul thirsts for You, our body longs for You, in a dry and weary land where there is no water. Rend the heavens. Come down. Meet us in this time of prayer. Etch into our hearts that the effectual, fervent prayer of a righteous person avails very, very much.

Let the way of the Lord be prepared. Let every high and arrogant thing be brought low. Let every low and oppressed thing be raised up. Let the crooked ways be made straight and rough places plain so that the glory of the Lord can be ushered back into Your Church and back into this city. Lord, we want to see Your glory. We claim Your Word, that if we, Your people, who are called by Your name would humble ourselves and pray and seek Your face, and turn from our wicked ways, then You would hear from heaven and forgive our sin and heal our land. Lord, Marietta, Atlanta and America desperately need healing.

Therefore, we humble ourselves and pray and seek Your face and turn from our wicked ways. Forgive us, Lord, of all our sins. Cleanse us by the precious blood of Jesus. Protect us by that same blood as we pray.

We cannot afford the luxury of resentment and bitterness. Right now, we lay it down. We repent of being lovers of pleasure more than lovers of God. We repent for lukewarmness and having made peace with mediocrity. Let the zeal of the Lord of hosts consume us. Let the Lord Jesus Christ become our magnificent obsession.

We repent of our unanointed religious exercises in futility. We repent of quenching the spirit and extinguishing His fire. We repent of having a form of godliness, but denying the power thereof. We repent of prayerlessness. Lord, we ask You to reduce us back down to the simplicity which is in Christ Jesus, and return the Church in Marietta back to its initial mandate. If it's known for anything, it will be known as a house of prayer for all nations.

We thank You, Lord, that Your people are coming out of bondage. We've been in captivity, under a cruel taskmaster, making bricks without straw long enough. We're taking our harps down from the willow trees. We're setting our face like flint. We're launching into the deep. We're burning our bridges behind us. We're putting our hand to the plow and we're not looking back. And, by the grace of God, we're going to dispossess the gates of the enemy, plunder the camp of darkness, and we're taking Cobb County back for the glory of God.

Lord, teach us how to pray. Raise up green-beret intercessor prayer warriors who are in their element when they pray, who know how to stand in the gap, make up the hedge, weep over a city, take hold of the horns of the altar, who won't take no for an answer, and will relentlessly take an assignment all the way to the gates.

Lord, we need You. Unless You do it, it's not going to happen. Unless the Lord builds the house, its builders labor in vain. Unless the Lord watches over the city, the watchmen stand guard in vain. Lord, we desperately need Your anointing this morning, that anointing which breaks the yoke, binds up the brokenhearted, brings freedom for captives, release for prisoners, comforts all who mourn, bestows on those who grieve a crown of beauty instead of ashes, the oil of gladness, instead of mourning, and a garment of praise instead of a spirit of despair.

Lord, there's enough spiritual firepower in this square to shake Marietta and Atlanta to its foundation. You said when we get in agreement, one of us shall put to flight a thousand, two—ten thousand, three—a hundred thousand, four—a million, seven—a billion. Everyone of us here in unity represents the decimal moving over one more to the right. There's not a super computer in America that has enough zeros to calculate this kind of power. It's awesome!

Therefore, in this solemn assembly, in the credible exponential power of corporate prayer agreement, with the protective blood of Jesus applied to our lives, we ask You these next few moments to transform us into a loving executive body to send forth decrees into the heavenlies that will not cease nor desist until You move here on earth, in Marietta, with awesome, supernatural power. Purge and cleanse this entire area by the blood of Jesus Christ. Send angels to help and protect us. This afternoon, let our enemy know he has met more than his match. Lord, move out as a valiant, conquering warrior in great conquest as the Lord strong and mighty in battle.

Drive out demonic beasts and everything that mutters and peeps and creeps and crawls. Let principalities and powers and territorial spirits gasp and crash and burn. Let there be a major shift in the heavenlies. Help us realize today the initiative is ours and the scepter is being placed back into our hands. Bring back Your majesty, Your grandeur, Your magnificence. Bring back Your glory. Let God arise and just as the smoke flees before the wind, and just as the wax melts before the fire, let His enemies be scattered. We thank You, Lord, when God arises, it's no contest. The enemy must be scattered.

Listen up, you spirit forces of darkness. This day, in the awesome power of corporate prayer agreement, we serve eviction papers on you. You may have come this far, but you're not coming any further. The Lord rebuke you. You will no longer run roughshod over God's people as if it were open season on Christians. The day is over that Cobb County and Atlanta are known as cities of crime and perversion. In the days to come they will be internationally famous as a safe haven, cities of refuge, and places where great revival is breaking out.

We decree and declare the Lordship and superiority and supremacy of Jesus Christ over this entire area of Marietta and Cobb County. We prophesy to the north, south, east and west. Come Holy Spirit of God. Fill this place with Your glory. Let us hear the rustling of Your garments on Interstates 75, 85, 285 and GA 400. Bring glory back into the Church. Bring glory back into this city. Let every resident in Cobb County know there's a God in Israel, there's a God in the United States of America, and there's a God over Marietta.

We thank You, Lord, that because of revival in prayer, that we are on the threshold of a historically, unprecedented spiritual awakening. We thank You, Lord, that homosexuals and lesbians, who have been so desperate for love and affection that they have been willing to sign a death warrant just to get a little affection, that a major revival is coming to them. We thank You, Lord, that the power of God is preparing to set them free. We thank You, Lord, some of the most anointed last day ministries are going to be raised up from the ranks of repentant, radically saved homosexuals.

We thank You, Lord, that if man refuses to bring his torch into Cobb County because we refuse to embrace a perverted lifestyle, then You're going to bring Your torch into Cobb County, the Holy revival fire of God. Bring it on!

We thank You, Lord, that where sin abounds, grace does much more abound.

We thank You, Lord, that though darkness covers the earth and gross darkness the people, that in direct proportion, as we speak, the light is brightly shining upon Your people.

We thank You, Lord, that what the enemy meant for evil, You are, as we speak, turning it for good. We thank You, Lord, that when the enemy comes in like a flood, You will raise up a standard against him. We thank You, Lord, when the enemy comes in, like a FLOOD You will raise up a standard against him.

We thank You, Lord, that You're about to do a thing in Marietta and Atlanta that will cause the ears of everyone who hears of it to tingle.

We thank You, Lord, that the day is coming when the knowledge of the glory of the Lord will fill the earth as the waters cover the sea. We thank You, Lord, that the glory of the latter house will greatly exceed that of the former.

We thank You, in Jesus' name, that You have saved the best wine 'til last.

God bless Marietta. God bless Atlanta and God bless America.

BEFORE WE PRAY · · ·

ଔ

From The Heart of an Intercessor consists of prayers gleaned from seven years of praying for the city of Atlanta every Monday morning on two Christian radio stations.

Looking back over this time, I realize it is an honor and responsibility to attempt to articulate the Father's heart for this world-class city. Jesus is our example when it comes to fervently interceding for the town where you live. He mounted the hill of Jerusalem, wept over the city, and prayed passionately with a note of desperation for that area.

"O Jerusalem, Jerusalem, you who kill the prophets and stone those sent to you, how often I have longed to gather your children together, as a hen gathers her chicks under her wings, but you were not willing. Look, your house is left to you desolate. For I tell you, you will not see me again until you say, 'Blessed is He who comes in the name of the Lord.'"
Matthew 23:37-39

There are two options for every city in America, as is made clear in this scripture. Either our house (spiritual and family) is left desolate, sinking deeper into degradation and wickedness, or through strong prevailing prayer and fasting, we see the tide turned, principalities and powers pulled down, and the glory and awesome anointed presence of the Lord ushered back into our churches, homes and society.

One of our primary burdens during these prayers has been to challenge the modern American church to be reduced back to the simplicity which is in Christ Jesus (2 Corinthians 11:3), and returned back to its initial mandate to be known as a "house of prayer for all nations" (Mark 11:17). This is accomplished by a "Jeremiah prayer anointing" which uproots, tears down, destroys and overthrows man's humanistic religion so the Lord can build and plant His true New Testament Church (Jeremiah 1:10).

The heart of an intercessor is graphically described in Lamentations 2:11-12. It is a picture of a fervent intervener who totally identifies with the heartbeat of the Father concerning the condition of their city.

"My eyes fail from weeping, I am in torment within, my heart is poured out on the ground because my people are destroyed, because children and infants faint in the streets of the city. They say to their mothers, 'Where is the bread and wine?' as they faint like wounded men in the streets of the city, as their lives ebb away in their mothers' arms."

What a picture of modern America!

God is presently raising up a special breed of intercessors. This is not just any generation. There is a portion of the remnant who have heard from God, consider it a critical mandate which at all costs must be carried out, do not want to compromise, and have opted to pay the price and take the high road. These are prayer warriors who have set their faces like flint, burned their bridges behind them, launched into the deep, put their hands to the plow and are not about to look back.

Realizing the present crucial hour of history, there is a note of urgency in these prayers for the church to awaken, reprioritize, shun that which is fleshly and religious, fervently seek the Lord in prayer, receive a fresh anointing, and pray in what we believe is going to be the greatest, unprecedented, historic spiritual awakening in the annals of history.

Special honor and thanks goes to my "Princess" wife, Lynn. During the last two years, she has been by my side every time I have prayed over the air for Atlanta. She is a powerful intercessor, and her standing with me, quietly pouring on the coals while I pray, has made more of a difference than I can put into words. One way of summing it up; "One shall put to flight a thousand, and two, ten thousand." Her faithful prayer support has resulted in an exponential increase in intercessory anointing which has impacted Atlanta.

May the mantle of intercession fall even more distinctly on you as you use these segments of prayer to intercede for your city.

**"The end of all things is near, therefore be clear minded
and self-controlled so that you can pray."**
I Peter 4:7

--David L. Thomas
(1939-2000)

CONFESSION AND REPENTANCE FOR THE CHURCH

○3

Dear Lord, we intercede for that which is dearest to Your heart, the Church of the Lord Jesus Christ. Come quickly, breathe upon it, because She, Your Bride, is in a weakened condition. A veil has been placed over Her eyes which is not the veil of the bride in her wedding chambers, but the veil of blindness. The enemy has rushed upon our city, run along the wall, climbed into the houses and like a thief has entered into the windows (Joel 2:9). Let God arise and the enemy be so scattered today, that this thief would be thoroughly dispelled as the glory of Your presence begins to flow over Your Church.

We ask You, Lord, that this prayer not be routine or ordinary. Paul stated in scripture that we are not to be mere men or women. By implication, we're not to conduct mere meetings or pray mere prayers. We pray, Lord, You would bring such conviction upon the American church, that we would no longer pump out meetings because it's 11 AM or 7:30 PM Sunday, but that we wouldn't make a move until the awesome majestic, magnificent presence of the Lord God of Israel shows up.

Lord, we are so weary of conjured-up, crowd-manipulating, mood music-motivated, performance-oriented, typical, bland, predictable, sterile, perfunctory church services which resemble being in a mausoleum. We humbly confess to You, we're so Americanized, so organized, so ecclesiastical, so well trained, such a product of our anemic seminaries, that we're going to have a meeting whether your presence is there or not. What a travesty! What flesh! What an abomination! What a stench in Your nostrils and for this we repent. Make it crystal clear to Your Church that we're not an organization; we're a Divine organism.

~~~~~
**"We humbly repent, as the American Church of neglecting the most underestimated dynamic power of this earth--prayer."**
~~~~~

Our hearts are burdened for the American Church. It's one thing for the ship to be in the water. It's quite another for the water to leak into the ship. And right now the Church is like a ship listing severely because the water of this world, doctrines of demons, the spirit of this age, and religious spirits have infiltrated the Church. We ask You, Lord, to burden intercessors all over this city to pray and continue to persevere in prayer until the Church sheds its "Americanized, sectarian version" of church and comes back to its roots and begins to resemble the New Testament Church, and begins to read like the Church in the book of Acts.

We humbly repent, as the American Church, of neglecting the most underestimated dynamic power of this earth--prayer. Forgive us, Lord, for going down to Egypt, wandering into Babylon, and bringing the world's principles into

2

the Church. We know this mixture is an abomination in Your eyes. Forgive us, Lord, for bringing into Your glorious Church the Babylonian, Egyptian principles of psychology, psychiatry, New Age, humanism and traditions of men, which make the Word of God of none effect and cause Ichabod to be written over our edifice doors.

Etch into our minds and spirits what church really is. Show Your people that it's not a building. It's from the Greek word "Ekklesia" meaning "called out ones." Show Your people that it's impossible for them to go to a building called church because the building is not the Church; but it is possible for Your Church, the "called out ones," to go to a building. Show Your people clearly that there is a difference between a civic club and the Church of the Lord Jesus Christ. Show Your people the difference between a secular organization and a spiritual organism.

"Let the priests, who minister before the Lord, weep between the temple porch and the altar. Let them say, Spare Your people, O Lord, do not make Your inheritance an object of scorn, a byword among the nations. Why should they say among the peoples, 'Where is their God?'"

Joel 2:17

When the gospel is preached, we pray that we would return back to New Testament norm, and let the Word be confirmed with signs following. Lord, forgive us for sitting around in our boring church services, singing the first, second and last. Forgive us for having organized the awesome presence, anointing and power of the Holy Spirit out of our gatherings.

We pray the heart cry of the Lord in Malachi 1:10.

"Oh, that one of you would shut the temple doors, so that you would not light useless fires on my altar! . . ."

3

We say, "Amen," to that scripture and away with useless man-made fires. In the place of that, ignite us with the fire of God like that which fell on Elijah's water-logged, soaked offering at the contest between God and 450 prophets of Baal and 400 prophets of Ashtaroth.

We repent, Lord, of our prayerlessness, of presuming on You by cranking out sterile religious meetings which are predictable and resemble the meeting before that one. We ask You to come by Your Spirit, remove the flesh, the carnality, the religious spirits and the traditions of men. Upset the status quo and burst upon the scene. God forbid that our religious machinery be found smoothly purring along and we be found "religiously correct," while we are naively oblivious to the fact that the candlestick has been extinguished; there is no more fire and Ichabod has been written over our door.

Lord, we don't want fanatical wildfire, but God knows we desperately need Your fire, the fire of Your ignited, inspired, quickened Word; the fire of holiness; the fire which will keep us from the jeopardy of being spewed out of Your mouth because we are lukewarm, neither hot nor cold. We confess we are so subnormal that when we do get a little Holy Ghost fire, most people think we have a temperature. Restore back to us a strong motivation and incentive to diligently seek Your face and to pursue You as a deer pants for streams of water.

Lord, do not be angry with us. Look upon us. Have mercy on Your people, Your bride, Your house.

"Your sacred cities have become a desert; even Zion is a desert, Jerusalem a desolation. Our holy and glorious temple where our fathers praised you, has been burned with fire, and all that we treasured lies in ruins."
Isaiah 64:10, 11

Judah mourns, our cities languish (Jeremiah 14:2). Desert creatures, hyenas, screech owls, and things that mutter and peep and creep and crawl have overrun Your house.

Lord, lift us out of our spiritually comatose state. Heal the Church from the frontal lobotomy which causes it to become a couch potato and require inordinate hours of entertainment, luxury, pleasure, amusement and pampering--even in the church. Forgive us for our spiritual malaise, for staggering around in a religious stupor. Forgive us for being like zombies. Jerk the slack out of the American Church and remind us that **"From the days of John the Baptist until now the kingdom of heaven suffereth violence, and the violent take it by force" (Matthew 11:12 KJV).**

Raise up a compassionate, loving, militant Church that will once again be respected in our society and by our adversary. Thank You that **"When a man's ways are pleasing to the Lord, he makes even His enemies live at peace with him" (Proverbs 16:7).**

We ask, You, Lord, to drop Your plumb line spoken of in Amos 7:7-9. Open our eyes to Your real New Testament Church. Forgive us for pontificating in Your name, conducting organizations and meetings and calling them "c-h-u-r-c-h," which oftentimes have little or no resemblance to what we read in the New Testament or the book of Acts. Forgive us, Lord, for adding to, taking away, altering, and causing it to fit our mold and our pre-conceived notions of what we think church should be. Forgive us for "Americanizing" New Testament Church. What a travesty! We realize if we were a corporation, we would be in court facing a heavy lawsuit for forgery and misrepresentation.

Lord, break us out of the monotonous, perfunctory routine of going to sterile, predictable religious meetings. We ask Your forgiveness for having made peace with mediocrity in

Your Church. Clean house once again. Bring back Your glory. Remove the shallow, the trite and flippant. Remove the hype and extravaganza. Remove the "Barnum and Bailey" atmosphere which has crept into the American Church. Remove the performance mentality and showmanship. Change us from a cheap, shallow Church to one which is glorious and majestic. Reduce us back down to the simplicity which is in Christ Jesus (2 Corinthians 11:3). Remove everything which hasn't been birthed by prayer in the Spirit and has no eternal value. Bring back Your holiness, Your grandeur and awesomeness. Bring back Your magnificence. Show this generation what church is all about.

Bring back a Godly jealousy to the Body of Christ as Paul expressed to the Corinthian church when they were led astray from their sincere and pure devotion to Christ. How could one of the enemy chase a thousand Christians or two of the enemy put ten thousand of Your people to flight unless their Rock had sold them, unless the Lord had given them up? Lord, reverse this condition. Once again, restore Your church so that one of Your people, having met Your simple conditions, will have the anointing to put to flight a thousand; two, ten thousand; three, one hundred thousand; four, one million; seven, one billion; and eight, ten billion. Reverse the balance of power back again firmly into the saints' camp.

~~~~~

"Lord, break us out of the monotonous, perfunctory routine of going to sterile, predictable religious meetings."

~~~~~

Help us, the Church, to be honest and get real. We ask You, Lord, to show us distinctly the contrast between soul and spirit. Prohibit us, Lord, any longer from conducting soulish, Americanized versions of church meetings. Etch into our brains and spirits that we have a mandate from the living God that we are to operate only in the realm of the Spirit. Give us a hunger for Your Word which is sharper than any two-edged sword and has the divine capacity to divide between soul and spirit.

There is a river which makes glad the city of God. Lord, we don't put a premium on ignorance. We don't ever want to be slothful concerning the resources You've given us. We want to develop our minds to the maximum and be diligent, but we pray that when people simply observe us, they would say the same about us as they said about Peter and John:

". . .they. . .realized that they were unschooled, ordinary men, they were astonished and they took note that these men had been with Jesus."

Acts 4:13

God, raise up intercessors to pursue the gates of heaven until the Dove descends on our gatherings, the fear of God enters our assemblies, holiness of the Almighty would be ushered in and time would go out the window. Let them pray until men, women and young people's hearts and consciences would be intensely pierced and stricken with conviction in the presence of a Holy God, so much so that they would be crying out to You over their sinful state, confessing their sins, contrite before God, and having their lives dramatically, radically transformed. Let it be that once again we would begin hearing Psalm 40:2, 3 testimonies:

"He lifted me out of the slimy pit, out of the mud and mire; he set my feet on a rock and gave me a firm place to stand. He put a new song in my mouth, a hymn of praise to our God. Many will see and fear and put their trust in the Lord."

Give us such a hunger, such an insatiable thirst for You, to seek Your face, to be in Your presence, to eat at Your table, drink at Your fountain, partake of Your bread, and devour Your Word, so much so that our priorities and schedules would be altered. Things that used to enamor us and take large blocks of our time would no longer occupy us. We would be mesmerized by You. As the old hymn of the faith says, **"The things of this world would go strangely dim in the light of Your Glory and grace."** Lord, we are serious about this. We ask You to exchange carnal, dissipating, deteriorating appetites for an insatiable appetite for You and everything that pertains to You. We want to be distracted by You. We want You to preempt our agendas. We want You to turn our heads. We want to be able to honestly say You are our magnificent obsession. As it was said about Jesus, let it be said about us, that the only consumption we have is that the zeal of the Lord of Hosts will consume us.

Come, Lord Jesus, breathe on this prayer. Let it be as is stated in Revelation 8:3-5, that our prayers be mixed with incense from Your altar and be hurled down on earth. We pray that Your will be done on earth as it is in heaven so that what is going on in the heavenlies, because of the prayers of the saints, will be hurled down on earth by the angels with such intensity that it will produce thunder, rumblings, flashes of lightning and shake the earth. Then, it will be manifested in Your Church and our lives in tangible, concrete ways--in healing, families, marriages, children, relationships, ministry, businesses and finances.

Thank You, Lord, that the effectual, fervent prayer of a righteous person avails much.

In Jesus' name, amen.

~2~

REVIVAL AND RESTORATION OF THE CHURCH

ભ

Lord, we ask You to prepare our hearts for the visitation of Your Spirit which has been promised in scripture. Like Daniel, when he discovered through the Word that the seventy years of desolation of Jerusalem would come to an end, he didn't just sit back and watch history roll. He entered into fervent, effectual, travailing prayer with all of his heart, to pray in the purposes, times and seasons of the Lord. So, Lord, help us by Your Spirit to do likewise.

We thank You, Lord, that there is something stirring in us that identifies with the loving, compassionate, righteous indignation of the Lord to pray impactful, dynamic prayers for Your beloved Bride, Your Church, to the extent that there will be set into motion something of Your Spirit that will light a fire, bring forth the Upper Room wind of Your Spirit, cause the river of life to flow, and move sovereignly as we have never witnessed You move before in our lifetime. We desperately need to experience firsthand the sovereign, majestic splendor of Your Holy presence, anointing and power. Let this be the year of Jubilee where captives are released and debts are forgiven.

We urgently pray, dear Lord, the inrushing of Your Spirit into a church body that threatens to become a corpse. Grant it that man and flesh and religion would retire into the background and let God take the field. Lord, make bare Your Holy arm and work in extraordinary power on saint and sinner. Bring Your Divine military strategy, first to counteract spiritual decline, and then to create spiritual momentum.

We pray for the Church of the Lord Jesus Christ in Atlanta and America. You love it beyond description. You died for it. It is blood-bought and blood-washed, and we pray today that You would light a spiritual fire under Your Church. Whatever it costs, we ask You, Lord, to bring a spiritual awakening, a Holy revival of the proportions, and even greater, than the first awakening in 1727, the second awakening in 1792, the third awakening or prayer revival in 1857, the fourth awakening in 1904, the Welsh revival in 1904, the latter rain movement in Canada in 1947, Azusa Street, and the renewal of the power and anointing and gifts of Your Holy Spirit which began in the 1960's and 1970's.

~~~~~
**"Bring a revival that will resemble a rocket that gets us back into orbit or New Testament Christianity."**
~~~~~

Bring a revival that will resemble a rocket that gets us back into orbit or New Testament Christianity. Lord, bring Your presence intensified, Your fullness, Your purposes accelerated. We ask You, Lord, to bring the first stage of revival--internal revival or renewal in which the Church would be set on fire and prodigals would begin to come home--en masse. Then, bring the second wave--external revival,

10

conversions of those outside the kingdom also on a mass scale. Heal Your Church so we can participate in a world-wide historic harvest. Bring widespread repentance both within the Church and among unbelievers.

We ask You, Lord, to replace the ecclesiastical, well-oiled religious machine called the modern day American Church which has a form of godliness but denies the power thereof, with old-fashioned, New Testament love, compassion, balance, authority, resurrection power, miracles, signs, wonders and demonstrations of Your omnipotence.

We pray as David did from a spiritually barren wasteland,

"O God, you are my God, earnestly I seek you; my soul thirsts for you, my body longs for you, in a dry and weary land where there is no water. I have seen you in the sanctuary and beheld your power and your glory."

Psalm 63:1,2

Those of us who have drunk at Your fountain, eaten from Your table, experienced Your presence--we are ruined forever. We will not be satisfied until we see You in the sanctuary, as David did, and behold Your power and glory. Lord, inspire Your intercessors to pray tenaciously until our gatherings are no longer predictable, boring, perfunctory and sterile, but they are so bathed in prayer, so ignited by the power of God, such intense conviction visits us, such an unction from God comes on anyone who dares to speak the Word of the Lord, such anointed praise ascends up to You that moves into high worship and warfare worship and we personally realize such a fearful presence of the living God.

We urgently ask You, Lord, to replace the cheapness, shallowness, triviality, the "Barnum and Bailey" atmosphere, humanistic psychology, fleshly self-help groups and therapy

11

sessions, the traditions of men which make the Word of none effect, religion--replace this tinkling cymbal and sounding brass with holiness, Godly statesmanship, magnificence, splendor, power, the awesome presence of the Lord, Your majesty, and a fresh anointing. Lord, bring back strong, piercing, intense conviction. Once again, let the Word not just be preached, but let it be preached as Paul said,

". . .not simply with words, but also with power, with the Holy Spirit and with deep conviction...."
1 Thessalonians 1:5

We ask You to remove the apathy from Your people, open our eyes to see the real condition of the Church and pray like there's no tomorrow until You restore it to a state of being a glorious Church. We thank You, Lord, that we are in a period of restoration. We thank You, Lord, You're not coming back for a hag or a bag lady--You're coming back for a beautiful, fragrant, winsome Bride without spot or blemish. And give us Your insight and perspective as You cleanse our lives from spots and blemishes in preparation for that glorious occasion.

Lord, instruct us in Your ways and Your methods. Your Word says that the people of Israel knew Your acts and Moses knew Your ways. We not only want to know Your acts, we want to know You personally, intimately, and un-learn the ways of religion which are riddled through and through with flesh and carnal Babylonian strategies of this world system. Reduce us back down to the simplicity which is in Christ Jesus (2 Corinthians 11:3). Like Samuel, give us such an opulent anointing that none of our words drop to the ground (1 Samuel 3:19).

Bring back Your awesome presence to the Church to the extent that once again we would experience the incredible drawing power and old-fashioned conviction of the Holy Spirit strangely moving upon the hearts of men. Cause it to read like the fifth chapter of Acts, that concerning the unbelievers, those who had no intentions of repenting or bowing their knee to You, they wouldn't even come close to the Church because they so respected and revered and feared the presence of the Lord.

We ask You this day to exchange carnal, ungodly, evil appetites for Godly appetites. Impart to us an insatiable thirst and hunger for righteousness to seek Your face. Let it be said of us as is stated in Psalm 42:1, 2.

"As the deer pants for streams of water, so my soul pants for you, O God. My soul thirsts for God, for the living God. When can I go and meet with God?"

Lord, we need revival. Let the fire fall. Let the wind of Your Spirit blow. Let our hearts burn hot for God.

"For Zion's sake I will not keep silent, for Jerusalem's sake I will not remain quiet, till her righteousness shines out like the dawn, her salvation like a blazing torch."

Isaiah 62:1

We pray to hasten the day that we will experience what it says in Haggai.

". . .'In a little while I will once more shake the heavens and the earth, the sea and the dry land. I will shake all nations, and the desired of all nations will come, and I will fill this house with glory,' says the Lord Almighty. 'The silver is mine and the gold is mine,' declares the Lord Almighty. 'The glory of this present house will be greater than the glory of the former house,' says the Lord Almighty. 'And in this place I will grant peace, declares the Lord Almighty.'"

Haggai 2:6-9

Thank You for the former house in which You, Lord, so filled it with Your presence that Moses could not stand to enter the Tent of Meeting because the cloud had settled upon it.

Thank You that the glory of the latter house is going to greatly exceed this.

God grant us this problem in the American Church that Your glory would be so thick, Your presence so awesome, Your Shekinah so intense, just like it was when Moses could not stand to enter the Tent of Meeting because the cloud had settled upon it, that it would take a concerted effort just to enter. We hold up to You the promise that in the latter days You ". . .will pour out your spirit on all flesh" (Joel 2:28 KJV). Not a single person will be exempt from at least having the opportunity to respond to this outpouring. Lord, we have never witnessed this in our lifetime. Make the Church today jealous of what we read about in the early awakening, the Welsh revival, and the book of Acts.

~~~~~

"Hasten the day that the knowledge of the glory of the Lord covers the earth just as the waters cover the sea (Isaiah 11:9)."

~~~~~

Hasten the day that the knowledge of the glory of the Lord covers the earth just as the waters cover the sea (Isaiah 11:9). Even though all logical reasoning and rationale scream out against the possibility of Your Church in America being restored like this, we resolutely stand fast on Your Word which is unchangeable, which is forever settled in heaven, which framed the universe and established the seas. We believe Your report. Whoever believes Your report, the arm of the Lord is going to be revealed to them. It's going to happen, even on a greater scale than this world has ever witnessed.

Help us to pray in the purposes and plans of God for our city. The day is soon coming that the initiative will be restored back to the Church. The ball will be in our court. We will act, the enemy will have to react and the scepter will once again be firmly placed back into our hands to wield under the wisdom, power and unction of the Holy Spirit.

Lord, we use the same terminology as used in scripture and pray in the beginnings of a revival of historic proportions. We pray in an "outpouring of the Spirit" (like rain or fire falling or wind blowing), "the renewing of God's mighty deeds" as spoken of in Habakkuk 3:2. We pray in "the glory of the Lord returning to Your temple," "God healing our land," and "the time of God's visitation" with Your manifest presence.

We pray for You, Lord, to come down as spoken of in Isaiah 64:1-4.

"Oh, that you would rend the heavens and come down, that the mountains would tremble before you! As when fire sets twigs ablaze and causes water to boil, come down to make your name known to your enemies and cause the nations to quake before you! For when you did awesome things that we did not expect, you came down, and the mountains trembled before you. Since ancient times no one has heard, no ear has perceived, no eye has seen any God besides you, who acts on behalf of those who wait for him."

"Let the priests, who minister before the Lord, weep between the temple porch and the altar. Let them say, 'Spare your people, O Lord. Do not make your inheritance an object of scorn, a byword among the nations. Why should they say among the peoples, 'Where is their god?'"

Joel 2:17

Help the Church to realize that either they stay so up-to-date with You and continually say, "Where is the Lord, what is

He doing?" or if they don't, the world will look at us and say, "Where is your God?"

We believe, Lord, just as You cleansed the temple in days of old, and then the blind and lame came to You and were healed, so as the Church is shaken and cleansed, there is coming on a wholesale basis, healing to the physical bodies of the members of Your Church.

Hasten the day that the Church in Atlanta would be returned back to its initial mandate and priority, that Your house, if it's known for anything, would be known as a house of prayer for all nations. Show us what church is and what it is not. We pray that multitudes who have been caught up in ecclesiastical exercises of futility which have no anointing nor any touch of God will turn from religion to relationship. Help us, members of the American Church, to realize Your Word which says:

"For the kingdom of God is not a matter of eating and drinking, but of righteousness, peace and joy in the Holy Spirit."
Romans 14:17

We hunger for Your presence. Let Your Word dwell in us richly; let the river of life flow freely through our midst. Take us out of a barren and parched land where no water is and bring us into a spacious land, a spiritual place which flows profusely with the river of life. Let not "Ichabod" be written across our assembly, but breathe a fresh breath upon us. Fill us with Your life-giving power.

Let our gatherings begin to resemble the Church in the book of Acts. When people think of the Word Church, let them not think of something routine or boring. Let them have an image of something magnificent and full of grandeur--something they can't wait to be a part of.

Lord, show us Your glory and that of Your Church. Let us familiarize ourselves with the Church triumphant. Let us walk about Zion, go around her, count her towers, consider well her ramparts, view her citadels--so we may tell it to the next generation--for this God is our God (Psalm 48:12-14).

We know that judgment begins at the house of God. Therefore Lord, we ask You to bring such a piercing light into Your Church that You would expose and cleanse from it that which makes it trivial, shallow, cheap, soulish, fleshly, carnal, worldly and religious, and bring back spiritual quality, a sense of reverence, holiness and magnificence. Bring it back to such a state that the world would be jealous for what we have, and we would find ourselves being ready to give an answer to those who ask us of the hope which is written all over our countenances (1 Peter 3:15).

Lord, bring back Your power, Your magnificence. Let Your Church resonate with grandeur, majesty and magnificence. Bring back Your glorious splendor.

"Blow the trumpet in Zion, declare a holy fast, call a sacred assembly. Gather the people, consecrate the assembly; bring together the elders, gather the children, . . ."
Joel 2:15-16

"You're ". . .about to do a thing in all the earth, that both ears of those who hear it will tingle" (1 Samuel 3:11).

We pray for You, Lord, to come down as spoken of in Isaiah 64:1-3.

"Oh, that you would rend the heavens and come down, that the mountains would tremble before you! As when fire sets twigs ablaze and causes water to boil, come down to make your name known to your enemies and cause the nations to quake before you! For when you did awesome things that we did not expect, you came down, and the mountains trembled before you. Since

17

ancient times no one has heard, no ear has perceived, no eye has seen any God besides you, who acts on behalf of those who wait for him."

The wind is blowing, there is a rustling of the Lord's garments and the sound of angels moving out on the wings of the wind. There is a voice coming from the mountain which says prepare the way of the Lord. Hasten the day. Rend the heavens and come down. Bring Your glory back to Your Church. Visit Your people once again.

Lord, let this be the year of Jubilee when captives are released and debts are forgiven. Once again, revive Your Church. We will pray till it happens. Give us the faith, the tenacity, the perseverance, the vision to press this battle to the gates.

In Jesus' name, amen.

RESTORATION OF THE ANOINTING TO THE CHURCH

CR

Dear Lord, bring back the anointing. Replace the mantle on our heads. Bring the essence and savor of the Holy Spirit into our lives. Let us not get involved in anything unless it is birthed of God through deep, prevailing, intercessory prayer. For it is that which is birthed of God that overcomes the world (1 John 5:4). Help us, Lord, once again to be known as overcomers. Increase that anointing savor that exudes from us, that ministers life to those who have the Spirit of life, and death to those who have demons of destruction--wherever we go (2 Corinthians 2:15-16).

"You who bring good tidings to Zion, go up on a high mountain. You who bring good tidings to Jerusalem, lift up your voice with a shout, lift it up, do not be afraid; say to the towns of Judah, 'Here is your God!" See, the Sovereign Lord comes with power, and his arm rules for him. . . ."

Isaiah 40:9-10

Increase that "Peter's shadow" anointing that whenever it fell on people, they were radically touched, healed, and delivered (Acts 5:15). It's not far fetched--You said greater things than these shall we do (John 14:12). So be it Lord!

We ask You to do a new thing in response to the prayers of Your people. Come and upset the status quo, move mountains, let it be different. Let it not be business as usual. Move through stalemates. Let the awesome anointing, the Shekinah glory of God come down upon us. We are hungry for more of You. We are thirsty for You as it says in Psalm 63:1,

"O God, you are my God, earnestly I seek you; my soul thirsts for you, my body longs for you, in a dry and weary land where there is no water."

Dear Lord, we celebrate today the resurrection power of Jesus Christ. We pray that everyday this year would be Easter in our hearts and that the life of the Lord would flow freely, profusely, unabated, unhindered, like a cascading river of pure water. We pray a fresh anointing in our lives. For those who have lost the lustre, the fervor, the zest, the enthusiasm of fellowshipping with You, we ask You to put us back on the cutting edge of walking in the Spirit and being up-to-date with what You are doing and saying. Help us to be like the children of Issachar who had an understanding of their times.

You are the God of the breakthroughs. You are the One Who can make everything new. You take away the stale and stagnant and bring that which is new, fresh and revitalizing. You are the One, Who with one stroke of Your hand, can banish far from us hopelessness and despair. Let Your anointing flow like a river.

In Jesus' name we pray. Amen.

~4~

RESTORATION OF SPIRITUAL AUTHORITY TO THE CHURCH

∝

Lord, we repent and ask forgiveness for our rebellion, prayerlessness and idolatry. Restore true, loving spiritual authority to the Church in Atlanta so that once again we would experience the exponential increase of power the way it was initially planned so that one of us would put to flight a thousand of the enemy; two, ten thousand; three, a hundred thousand; four, a million; and seven, a billion. Help us to realize the incredible spiritual firepower that is available to us so that every time a brother or sister agrees with us in prayer, the decimal is moved over one. Lord, give us this kind of decimal, decimating power. Raise up these kinds of intercessors and prayer groups in our city.

Lord, help us to cease and desist from acting beggarly and constantly being on the defensive. Quicken to us what you really did on the cross of Calvary when you divested and stripped satan of his authority and made an open show of him (Colossians 2:15). Help us to enforce the victory that has already been won at Calvary. Lord, You have given us the land that flows with milk and honey which also has giants-- Canaanites, Jebusites and Hittites. Give us the grace to

21

decisively take the land which You have so freely given to Your people.

We pray this morning to restore balance and integrity into the Body of Christ. We pray that the Church will no longer be anemic, nor powerless, nor a laughingstock, nor resemble the seven sons of Sceva who mouthed words, but lacked the spiritual authority to back up the words, and in their confrontation with the adversary, ran out of the house severely beaten. Restore Your Church, Lord Jesus, to the extent that we would operate in such wisdom and authority that not even our enemies would be able to withstand nor gainsay or resist and they would be forced to respect us (Luke 21:15).

God, give us prayer warriors who will not make peace with mediocrity, who have keen discernment, can smell a religious spirit a mile away, and will never again waste their precious time in unanointed religious exercises in futility. Give us ones whose heads are not turned by the smell of money, who have no price tags hanging off them--they can't be bought, leveraged, manipulated or controlled. Intercessors, who when they go out to the battlefield, have spiritual authority on their head because they're under authority and are covered by their local church body. Thank You for restoring loving authority and hearing our prayer.

In Jesus' name, amen.

~5~

REMOVAL OF
APATHY
FROM THE CHURCH

CR

Lord, visit an apathetic, complacent, arrogant American Church. Have mercy upon us and even if we don't deserve it, we humbly ask You to extend Your grace and give us more time. At whatever the cost, whatever we have to sacrifice, we ask You to send a spiritual awakening of such magnitude and proportion that this world has never known. It's our only hope.

Lift us out of our spiritually comatose state. Heal the Church from the frontal lobotomy which causes it to become a couch potato and require inordinate hours of entertainment, luxury, pleasure, amusement and pampering--even in our church meetings. Forgive us for our spiritual malaise and for staggering around in a religious stupor. Forgive us for being like zombies.

Help us, Lord, Your Church, to awaken out of our state of deep, hypnotic slumber, clothe ourselves with Your strength, shed our miserly, miserable rags, put on Your garments of splendor, shake off the dust, rise up and sit enthroned (Isaiah 52:1, 2). We pray this day that many of Your people that have been in a spiritually slouched position will rise up, sit enthroned and we ask You Lord, this day, to be the glory and lifter of their heads. Wash from us the apathy and complacency which is rampant in our society and in the Church. Let it not have its deadening, stupefying effect on us.

Forgive us for breathing in the anesthesia of this world system. Forgive us for drinking at the cesspools of humanism and relying on the brilliant, bankrupt think tanks of our day. Forgive us, Lord, for being mesmerized into a state of spiritual slumber while a well-disciplined, invading enemy army, like insects has crept over our walls, into our windows, invaded our homes and taken our children while we have been asleep. Lord, jolt us out of our slumber. The Church of the Lord Jesus Christ has received the greatest wakeup call in decades: this last Presidential election *[1996]*. God forbid that we should press the snooze button.

Deliver the Church from the average, typical, nominal, traditional western American Church mindset. We repent for our plans of self-aggrandizement while the world perishes. Forgive us for heaping upon us more gadgets, trinkets, toys, and more comforts so we can increase our leisure time and inordinately titillate and indulge the flesh. Impart to us Your attribute of zeal spoken of in Isaiah 42:13.

"The Lord will march out like a mighty man, like a warrior he will stir up his zeal; with a shout he will raise the battle cry and will triumph over his enemies."

We pray this in Jesus' name. Amen.

~6~

CLEANSING
OF THE CHURCH

൦ൟ

Dear Lord, we confess that the new wine of Your Spirit has become diluted and lost its lustre, vibrancy and pulsating power. Lord, we submit ourselves to You to cleanse, purge and purify us by the blood of Jesus and the washing of the Word. Remove the mixture, the impurities, the dilution which has reduced the new wine's potency and the Church's spiritual dynamics. Let it not be said of us as God exhorted Israel,

"Your silver has become dross, your choice wine is diluted with water."
Isaiah 1:22

Let it never be said again that we dilute the pungency, potency and power of Your Holy Spirit with man's methods and strategies. We hunger for the day when once again we can experience the New Testament dynamics and resurrection power.

Lord, we cannot express to You how exceedingly grateful we are to You. In a dirty, contaminated, polluted society where the gates of putrefaction have been opened by the Supreme Court and brilliant intellectual leaders in our nation have introduced raw sewage and immorality to our society and

25

youth--in the midst of all this, we can experience Your purity, Your wholeness, Your holiness and Your cleansing. For this, we will praise You morning, noon and night. We ask You to bring back old-fashioned holiness, old-fashioned righteousness, and old-fashioned purity.

We beseech You, Lord, to make Your Church holy. Cleanse her ". . .by the washing with water through the word, . ." so she can be presented to You ". . .as a radiant church, without stain or wrinkle or any other blemish" (Ephesians 5:26-27). Give us Your perspective, grace, understanding, patience, and forbearance as You apply the fire of Your Spirit to smooth out the wrinkles in our lives. Let the way of the Lord be prepared so You can, once again, usher in Your glory and Your house will be known as a glorious, majestic Church.

We ask You to help us to separate the precious from the vile and to make a distinction between the holy and unholy so we can utter worthy, not worthless words, and so be Your spokesman (Jeremiah 15:19).

Let God arise. We thank You, Lord, that we are made clean by Your Word. We thank You for Your Word in Psalm 119:9 which we claim for our children.

"How can a young man keep his way pure? By living according to your word."

We thank You for Your Word in John 15:3.

"You are already clean because of the word I have spoken to you."

"Sanctify them by the truth; your word is truth."
                                                          John 17:17

Thank You, Lord, we are made clean by the Word. Thank You for the blood of Jesus Christ and for answering our prayer.

In Jesus' name we pray. Amen.

~7~

PROCLAMATION OF
THE FULL GOSPEL
IN THE CHURCH

CR

Lord, forgive us for having an apologetic attitude toward what You did while on earth and what we read in scriptures. We pray to raise up ministry which is anointed by Your Spirit, who have no fear of man, who themselves are baptized in the Holy Spirit and will not deprive Your people of personal power. Raise up leaders who will encourage Your people into a truly Spirit-filled life.

Lord, Your Word says that if You cast out demons by Your finger, then know that the kingdom of God has been visited upon us (Luke 11:20). Raise up ministry who will not capitulate on this issue, who do not have blood on their hands, as Paul said, because they do not fail to proclaim the whole counsel of God (Acts 20:27), but who will be willing to become controversial and if necessary bear reproach and be stigmatized. But, in any case, they will have the courage and the presence of the Lord to pray deliverance prayers and cast demons out of Your people that are driven, enslaved, enticed, tormented and compelled.

Forgive us for ever having scorned or snubbed the gifts of Your Holy Spirit. We willingly embrace them--including discernment and discerning of spirits. Lord, give us words of wisdom and words of knowledge. Bring back Your miracles. Lord, remove from the Church doctrines of demons which deprive Your people of power, anointing and deliverance. Remove far from us the teaching that these things were only for the days of the apostles. Etch into our spirits what it says in Hebrews that **"Jesus Christ is the same yesterday, today and forever" (Hebrews 13:8).**

Remove from us the teachings of dispensationalism which deprive Your people today of the power and deliverance and miracles which they so desperately need to be overcomers. Quicken to our spirits what is said in scripture--greater things than these (that Jesus did) shall we do (John 14:12). Lord, bring Your glory and power back into the Body of Christ. Remove hirelings and raise up leadership who will declare the whole counsel of God.

Lord, we again ask Your forgiveness for taking Your precious Word and coming up with an "Americanized version" of it. Help the Church to realize they are not to tamper with Your infallible, inspired Word. Help us to responsibly carry Your gospel in all of its totality, not adding to nor leaving anything out. And we take seriously the admonition in Revelation 22:19.

"And if anyone takes words away from this book of prophecy, God will take away from him his share in the tree of life and in the holy city, which are described in this book."

In Jesus' name we pray. Amen.

8

RESTORATION OF INITIATIVE TO THE CHURCH

 os

In the place of perfunctory, mundane, anemic, boring meetings, we ask dear Lord, to turn the Church of the Lord Jesus Christ in this city into an executive body which will corporately decree a thing, catapult forth that decree into the heavenlies and see the staggering, mind-boggling extrapolation of exponential decimal decimating prayer power--one of us will put to flight a thousand; two, ten thousand; and four, a million.

We pray that once again in history, a second-rate diabolical power which for decades has run rough-shod over the Church as if it were open season on Christians, would all of a sudden realize that his satanic highness has met more than his match, is having eviction papers served on him, reels backward in abject panic and horror, and is routed out of this city into dry places to await the Judgment Day. Let it be that once again the Church has the initiative, the scepter is placed firmly in its hands, the ball is in its court, the Church speaks and demonic nobilities must listen.

Deliver us, Lord, from being a reactionary Church. Let the rod of authority be so firmly planted in our hands that we, under the guidance of Your Spirit, set the agenda and the prince of the power of the air would so be held hostage by your prayer warriors that he would have no option except to follow that agenda. Help us, the Church, to so repent of our evil deeds, and be up-to-date with You on our forgiveness, that we would once again have the initiative. We would act and the adversary would be forced to react.

We pray that the Church will no longer be anemic, nor powerless, nor oblivious to spiritual warfare, nor a laughingstock, nor resemble the seven sons of Sceva who mouthed words but lacked the spiritual authority to back up the words and in their confrontation with the adversary, ran out of the house severely beaten. Restore Your Church, Lord Jesus, to the extent that we would operate in such wisdom that not even our enemies would be able to withstand nor gainsay and they would respect us.

Lord, we ask You to restore such respect, honor and statesmanship to the Body of Christ that it would be like it was in Acts 5:11-14.

"Great fear seized the whole church and all who heard about these events. The apostles performed many miraculous signs and wonders among the people. . .No one else dared join them, even though they were highly regarded by the people. Nevertheless, more and more men and women believed in the Lord and were added to their number."

In Jesus' name we pray. Amen.

9

RESTORATION OF INTIMACY WITH THE LORD IN THE CHURCH

∞

Re-instill into us, Lord, such a passion to seek Your face, eat Your Word, drink at Your fountain, banquet at Your table, to come aside and enter into Your inner-sanctum, to enter into the Holy of Holies with You, that like David, we will hardly be able to wait and will say, "When can we come and spend intimate time with You?" Lord, let us so experience this that the hours with You and Your Word would seem like minutes.

Impart to us, Lord, an insatiable thirst for close, intimate fellowship with You likened unto that which Adam and Eve experienced in the Garden in the cool of the day as they walked and talked with You. Restore back to us the excitement and enthusiasm of eating by the hour at Your table. Help us to see the picture of You standing at the door and knocking, longingly waiting for us to hear Your voice, opening the door, inviting You in and having sweet communion with You. Let it be said of us that the Lord Jesus Christ is our magnificent obsession.

For those who either have not or in a long time have not personally experienced the inexpressible joy of fellowshipping with You in an intimate way like this, waiting upon You, reveling

33

in Your Word by the hour, who have not experienced a mighty rushing river running through their innermost being to cleanse, fill, soothe and satisfy--let the waters flow, let the showers begin to fall. Bring on the early and latter rain. We pray that out of their innermost being will flow rivers of living water--that river which makes glad the city of God.

Give us the incentive to delight ourselves in You, and as we do, You said You would give us the desires of our heart. There are some out there who are trying to get their own desires without delighting themselves in You. Give us a renewed, increased hunger to seek Your face, to have night seasons with You, to initiate a quest to diligently pursue You as never before. We pray for businessmen out there who are extremely disciplined and enterprising in pursuing and capturing new business, that they would be as diligent and disciplined in seeking You as if they were seeking silver and gold.

Help Your people to realize that in Your presence is fullness of joy and at Your right hand are pleasures forever more. Show them that in comparison, the pleasures and playthings of this world are but a hollow shadow in contrast to the deep, lasting fulfillment and substance You have to offer. Turn those who are listening from flighty, trivial, shallow, empty humans into persons of substance and honor.

We pray this in Jesus' name. Amen.

~10~

"NO LONGER"
TOLERATING THE ENEMY
IN THE CHURCH

ભ

Plant in our hearts, dear Lord, a jealousy for the Church, to the extent that no longer would New Testament principles be reversed; no longer would it be said that our Rock has sold us because of our sins and hardness of heart. No longer would one of the enemy put to flight a thousand of Your people; or two, ten thousand; but reverse the curse so that once again one of Your people would put to flight a thousand of the enemy; two, ten thousand; three, a hundred thousand; four, one million; seven, a billion; and eight, ten billion. Revive Your Church!

Paul said in First Corinthians 3:3, that we are not to be mere people, and by implication, we are not to have mere meetings. Lord, we need nothing less than a Divine visitation from on high to preempt our sterile, predictable assemblies. We no longer want any part of ecclesiastical exercises in futility. The world chuckles at our little religious serenades. The young generation, for the most part, has gotten bored and many have gone to a second-rate power. We claim Your scripture in Habakkuk 3:2.

"Lord, I have heard of your fame; I stand in awe of your deeds, O Lord. Renew them in our day, in our time make them known; in wrath remember mercy."

The day is soon coming that no longer will church be boring; no longer will people be looking at their watches; no longer will they become restless Sunday morning; no longer will our services be limited to just what's on the bulletin; no longer will services be predictable; no longer will they pump out sterile powerless meetings; no longer will they try to put the Holy Spirit in a straitjacket and quench Him; no longer will they put out the Spirit's fire; no longer will they despise and prohibit prophecy.

We pray for our young generation, that no longer will they leave the Church in droves because of its impotency and dullness. We pray that their entire concept, image and connotation of the Word Church would be revolutionized in their minds. Let it be that when they hear the Word, they would no longer think of an ecclesiastical edifice with a steeple, but there would instantly be brought to their mind the "ekklesia," the "called out ones," the Body of Christ which is living, moving, and being borne along by the glory of God and the power of Your Spirit. Let them hear once again the awesome mighty rushing wind, the same wind which visited the Upper Room. Lord, move so mightily upon Your Church in these days of restoration that our children would **"count her towers, consider well her ramparts, and view her citadels" (Psalm 48:12, 13).**

Visit us, Lord, with Your power, Your might and a fresh anointing. Bring back Your glory to Your Church so the reproach can be wiped away. Let our children no longer chuckle at a first-rate power that is being held hostage by a second-rate power. Hasten the day that it will not be commonplace for Your people, who are called by Your name, to fall like flies and be run over rough-shod by disease, darkness and death. But once again, let there be a resurgence of might, a demonstration of Your power and deliverance. Let healing power once again flow freely into the walking wounded, the pain-racked bodies and the desperate. By Your anointing, break the bands of wickedness and the death sentence from Your hurting people. Restore health, prosperity and peace.

We pray that the Church will no longer be anemic, nor powerless, nor oblivious to spiritual warfare, nor a laughingstock, nor resemble the seven sons of Sceva who mouthed words, but lacked the spiritual authority to back up the words and in their confrontation with the adversary, ran out of the house severely beaten. Restore Your Church, Lord Jesus, to the extent that we would operate in such wisdom that not even our enemies would be able to withstand nor gainsay it, and they would be forced to respect us. Help us to realize that as we repent and diligently seek Your face, the initiative is ours, the ball is in our court. We act and darkness must react.

Dear Lord, we pray that no longer will the Holy One of Israel be exasperated and frustrated; no longer will the eternal purposes of God for His Church from the foundations of the world be thwarted; no longer will the wind of Your beautiful Spirit be diverted from our assemblies; no longer will the precious Holy Spirit stay far away from our gatherings because of being unwelcome, and

~~~~~

"Restore Your Church, Lord Jesus, to the extent that we would operate in such wisdom that... even our enemies... would be forced to respect us."

~~~~~

made to feel like an orphan or estranged; no longer will sin and immorality be tolerated; no longer will Jezebel pontificate behind the scenes controlling and inhibiting leadership.

We pray that no longer will Your Bride, the Church, use Madison Avenue and Wall Street techniques to try to further their cause; no longer will lost people be able to come into services and leave lost without coming under intense, piercing conviction of the Holy Spirit.

Lord, move so among leadership that no longer will members tolerate dynasties of controlling pastors; no longer will ministers who have strong dominating personalities lead through subtle intimidation; no longer will church eldership tolerate controlling pastors who are nothing more or less than benevolent dictators.

We pray that no longer will Your Church resemble the seven sons of Sceva, naïve and nearly oblivious to spiritual warfare and when there's a confrontation, run out of the house beaten and wounded. No longer will pastors pump out services just because it's 11 AM or 7 PM Sunday, regardless of whether the Holy Spirit shows up or not; no longer will the Church be full of hype and performance; no longer will worship leaders try to generate and manufacture worship and praise; no longer will it be difficult or nigh impossible to distinguish between the world and the Church.

We pray this morning that no longer will there be an ignorance among the majority of Your people concerning what the anointing really is. No longer will we perpetuate fraud among Your people by misrepresenting to Christians and their children a sterile, impotent version of "Americanized" Church which has practically no resemblance to what we read about in the New Testament and the book of Acts. No longer will there be cranked out, unanointed messages which give Your people more head knowledge and outlines and do nothing to radically transform lives. No longer will there be presentations from our pulpits which are nothing more than the letter of the law which kills without the anointing of Your Spirit which gives life. No longer will there be a regimented presentation of scripture verses, outlines and notes without the corresponding quickening to impact the listeners and bring forth much fruit.

We pray, dear Lord, for Your beloved Church, that no longer will it be run over rough-shod by demon armies as spoken of in Joel, easily uninhibitedly charging over our city walls, into our homes and terrorizing Your people, tormenting, harassing, pillaging and plundering as if it were open season on Christians, without being intercepted and thrown backward. Dear Lord, no longer allow Christian businessmen to become more astute and learned in the latest state of the art technology and at the same time, be spiritual ignoramuses when it comes to God's Word, spiritual warfare, covering their families and the things of God. No longer allow our adversary to rip us off in broad daylight without strong intercession which would arrest him in his tracks and force him to restore back to Your people at least seven fold.

We pray, dear Lord, that no longer would Christians be ignorant and naïve as to where we are in history, what time it is on the Lord's time-table, and what season we're in and what to do about it; no longer would Christians trivialize and waste precious time, but realize the urgency of the hour, gird up the loins of their mind and let the zeal of the Lord accomplish all of this. Thank You for hearing our prayer.

In Jesus' name, amen.

RESTORATION OF SPIRITUAL POWER IN THE CHURCH

ભ

Dear Lord, we humbly confess to You the state of the Church in America and our own condition. We are anemic, impotent, to a large degree powerless and have become a laughingstock to many.

Help us to realize what it says in 2 Corinthians 3:6, that the **". . .letter killeth, but the Spirit giveth life" (KJV).** And what Paul said in First Corinthians 4:20 that **". . .the kingdom of God is not a matter of talk but of power."** And what he said in First Corinthians 1:17, **"For Christ. . ."** sent me **". . .to preach the gospel, not with words of human wisdom, lest the cross of Christ be emptied of its power."** And First Corinthians 2:4, **"My message and my preaching were not with wise and persuasive words, but with a demonstration of the Spirit's power."**

Lord, we need more than sermons, outlines, charts, notes, seminars and therapy sessions. We need a modern day demonstration of Your power that will leave us breathless, with our mouths wide open, awestruck and smitten, something that will indelibly impact our lives and the lives of our children forever.

How could a second-rate power, which is much weaker than You, ever, even for a season, run rough-shod over Your Church except that we have become a nation without sense and discernment? How could one chase one thousand; two put ten thousand to flight, unless their Rock had sold them, unless the Lord had given them up? (Deuteronomy 32:30) How could our new wine which is so potent and powerful become like grapes filled with poison, clusters filled with bitterness and our wine become the venom of serpents and the deadly poison of cobras except we have become a nation without sense and discernment and been sold to our enemies? (Deuteronomy 32:32-33)

Let there be a paradigm shift in the heavenlies and a first-rate power be returned to a position of superiority over a second-rate power. We call upon You, Lord, this morning. We desperately need Your power. Reveal Your right arm. Show Yourself strong on behalf of Your praying people.

As Paul prayed, we ask You to give us the spirit of wisdom and revelation, so that we may know You better. We pray that the eyes of our heart may be enlightened in order that we may know the hope to which we are called, the riches of Your glorious inheritance in the saints, and Your incomparably great power to us who believe (Ephesians 1:17-19). Thank You for hearing our prayer.

In Jesus' name we pray. Amen.

~ 12 ~

RESTORATION OF INTERCESSION IN THE CHURCH

ᔢ

Dear Lord, we ask that prayer will no longer be trivialized in our churches, glossed over, treated in a perfunctory manner, and put on the back burner as non-essential. Adjust our priorities, that once again Your Church will be known as a house of prayer for all nations. Do away with the reproach and the stigma which has been attached to us. Let us no longer be a laughingstock, a hissing, a byword, or a conversation piece to be bantered about by society.

We ask You, Lord, to jolt the Church out of its state of slumber and lethargy. We pray in a deep resolve to never again hold another meeting that is not bathed in prayer before, during, and after. Grant that our gatherings would begin to resemble the New Testament Church and the assembly in the book of Acts.

We acknowledge before You this day, Lord, we have only two options: Your Church shall either become a den of thieves and robbers, or it shall be a house of prayer. We invite You to cleanse Your temple, drive out that which robs, steals, perverts, distorts and dilutes.

Strengthen the hands and hearts of the intercessors in this area to rise up and prevail upon You for the Church victorious and the Church militant to come forth in all of its glory, radiance, authority and power to take back this area for the purposes for which it was originally intended. Bring back the glory to Your Church, so once again, our assemblies can begin to resemble the New Testament and read like the book of Acts.

~~~~~

"Give us such a love for Your Church that at times we could mount the hill of our city and weep intercessory tears over Your Bride."

~~~~~

It's obvious, Lord, You have come back to cleanse the temple just as You did in New Testament days when Your house of prayer had deteriorated into a merchandising market. We acknowledge Your Church is either a safe haven for thieves and robbers where Christians get ripped off, or it's a house of prayer for all nations. Bring back a mantle of prayer. Let us identify with the Father's heartbeat. Let us pray the Father's prayers. God, restore us back to New Testament Church. Increase our hunger for You and give us an insatiable thirst for Your Word.

Give us such a heart of compassion for Your Church-- just like You, Lord Jesus, when You cried out in Matthew 23:37.

"O Jerusalem, Jerusalem, you who kill the prophets and stone those sent to you, how often I have longed to gather your children together, as a hen gathers her chicks under her wings, but you were not willing."

Give us such a love for Your Church that at times we could mount the hill of our city and weep intercessory tears over Your Bride. Raise up prayer warriors who will so identify with the Father's heart and pray the Father's prayers over the Church in this city and press in and persevere until religious demons are routed, doctrines of devils are silenced and ecclesiastical hirelings who are building self-aggrandizing dynasties are replaced with those who have a true shepherd's heart which is full of love and will feed Your sheep.

We pray that You would raise up an army of intercessors, green-beret prayer warriors who are loving and kind, but also tenacious, persistent and persevering, who will take an assignment by Your Spirit and press it to the gates and won't take "No" for an answer. Lord, in the midst of all of our organization and board meetings and therapy sessions and anemic churchianity, we desperately need those who know how to stand in the gap and make up the hedge, who know how to take hold of the horns of the altar, and weep between the altar and the porch as spoken of in Joel, and pray until the atmosphere is charged with the presence of the Lord. Thank You for restoring prayer back to Your Church.

In Jesus' name we pray. Amen.

~ 13 ~

DEALING WITH "RELIGION" IN THE CHURCH

❧

We ask You, Lord, to remove from us religious exercises of futility. Spare us from traditions of men which make the Word of God of none effect. Remove far from us ecclesiastical involvements which have no anointing and matter nothing for eternity. Save us from liturgical emptiness which has a form of godliness but denies the power thereof (2 Timothy 3:4-5) and reduce us back down to the simplicity which is in Christ Jesus (2 Corinthians 11:3). Let God arise, and when God arises, there's no contest. The only option the enemy has is to be scattered. Let God arise and just like smoke is blown away by the wind, may You blow them away; as wax melts before the fire, may the wicked perish before God (Psalm 68:1, 2).

To whatever degree we have allowed the Church to become religious, we repent and ask forgiveness. God deliver us from stale, stagnant, mundane, lifeless, boring, perfunctory, predictable religion and descend upon Your people like You did in the Upper Room. Let the same wind blow as it did then. We need a fresh visitation. We need the Dove of Your Spirit to descend upon us. We need to hear from the Lord. Our children need to see with their own eyes what New Testament Church is really like.

Lord, we are serious. Whatever it takes, we pray for a Jeremiah anointing to root out, pull down, destroy and overthrow that which is religious, fleshly and ecclesiastical, so that You can build and plant Your true New Testament Church (Jeremiah 1:10). Let the Church in Atlanta begin to read like the Church in the Book of Acts. Therefore, in the authority of the unchanging Word of the living God, we ask You to root out spirits of religion, sectarianism, humanistic psychology, co-dependent groups, therapy sessions, etc., etc., and reduce the Church back down to the simplicity which is in Christ Jesus and return us back to our primary calling and initial mandate, that if we are known for anything it is to be a house of prayer for all nations (Mark 11:17). Change the Church from religion to intimate relationship with their God.

~~~~~

"God spare Your people from the hectic, frenzied, fast-paced activity of empty, sterile, hollow religious activities."

~~~~~

We pray for religious people, that they would forsake their dead, dull, boring, perfunctory religion and cease wasting time in ecclesiastical exercises in futility and come into an intimate, passionate, vital, living relationship with the Lord Jesus Christ. We pray as David did in Psalm 63:1, 2 (AMP).

"O God, You are my God; earnestly will I seek You; my inner self thirsts for You, my flesh longs and is faint for You, in a dry and

weary land where no water is. So I have looked upon You in the sanctuary, to see Your power and Your glory."

Lord, shut down dead meetings. Bind up religious spirits in this city and bring a fresh visitation of Your Holy Spirit. We are thirsty and hungry to experience what happened in the Early Awakening and the Welsh revival. We pray that the Church would begin to read once again like the New Testament and the Church in the book of Acts.

Remove far from us any vestige of religion. God spare Your people from the hectic, frenzied, fast-paced activity of empty, sterile, hollow religious activities. Impart to us an unprecedented disdain for anything religious. We hunger for that which has the depth and substance and fullness and fragrance of Your Spirit resident in it.

We recoil backwards from that which is ecclesiastical, has absolutely no anointing, but does have the sound of tinkling cymbal and sounding brass. We pray that Your people would be able to distinguish between the two and no longer tolerate such a travesty, such misrepresentation, such counterfeiting of the real thing. We realize if we were guilty of this kind of misrepresentation in the business world, we would be indicted for fraud, misrepresentation and have our hands full of lawsuits. Help Your people to be wary of and flee spirits of religion, enticement or seduction, nor listen to the appealing siren songs of this world system. We will never be reduced to low living again--ever. We choose to take the high road.

Forgive us for being apologetic or trying to improve on what Jesus did while He was on this earth. Forgive us for dividing Your Body into compartments. Bring us to a place of prayer power where we can serve eviction papers on spirits of divisiveness, religion and sectarianism which for ages have fragmented the Church of the Lord Jesus Christ. You paid the eternal price. You died to tear down walls of perdition and every other wall of division. Your Word says in John 13:35,

"By this all men will know that you are my disciples, if you love one another."

Remove the spirits of divisiveness and sectarianism so that we can love one another and then the world will know that we are Your disciples. We pray for an unprecedented unity into Your Church which will strengthen our prayer power.

Draw a clear line of demarcation between the Church and the world. Let them not be blurred so that once again there would be a clear distinction between the two. Let not the Church be run like a secular organization with its worldly structures, but let it once again move forth in New Testament love, authority and let it be a spiritual organism with life, zest, creativity, prophetic word, and prayers that avail much.

Deliver us from routine, mundane, shallow, cheap, perfunctory, superfluous, mechanical, ecclesiastical exercises which are rife with flesh, that not only accomplish nothing, but often reek of religious spirits. Bring our assemblies into a realm of ministry to the Lord to such a degree that once again You see fit to bring back Your awesome presence and usher us into a place of reverence, holiness, splendor, and majesty where we can savor Your magnificence and tremble as we realize we are actually standing upon Holy ground. We hunger for You, Lord, to be our place of habitation and to see fit to tabernacle amongst us. Quicken to us what it really means that Your address is praise and worship, that You abide in the praises of Your people.

In the name of Jesus, we pray. Amen.

~14 ~

REPENTANCE
IN THE CHURCH

∞

Dear Lord, bring us to our senses.   Let there be an awakening, first of all for the Church since judgment begins at the house of God, and let us come and reason together. Though our sin of the lack of the fear of God be as scarlet, we can be as white as snow in Your righteousness.

Forgive us for lounging on our couches of comfort and laps of luxury while a second-rate power runs over us roughshod as if it were open season over the Church, our homes, our marriages, children, and loved ones.

We repent of our unanointed religious exercises in futility. We repent of quenching the Spirit and extinguishing His fire. We repent of having a form of godliness but denying the power thereof. We repent of prayerlessness.   Lord, we ask You to reduce us back down to the simplicity which is in Christ Jesus and return the Church back to its initial mandate. If it's known for anything, it will be known as a house of prayer for all nations.

We repent of having reduced the glorious, majestic Church of the Lord Jesus Christ to a crust of bread by cheapening it with the anemic, powerless shallow methods,

51

tactics and strategies of this world system. Forgive us, Lord, for bringing humanistic, secular ideas into Your beautiful Bride. Forgive us for bringing Madison Avenue techniques into Your Body. Forgive us for being known as a house of self-help groups, co-dependent societies, recovery groups, a place of religious, man-made fabricated activities and not as a house of prayer.

We repent of being a slumbering, apathetic, complacent Church that has created a spiritual vacuum into which has rushed diabolical powers of darkness. We repent of being in a state of malaise and spiritually comatose while an inferior power has run roughshod over a superior power--the Church of the Lord Jesus Christ. We repent of our religious exercises in futility which have lacked anointing and spiritual power. We repent of playing Church while things that mutter and peep and creep and crawl have infiltrated the Body of Christ.

~~~~~

"We repent of our religious exercises in futility which have lacked anointing and spiritual power."

~~~~~

We repent of allowing the enemy to overrun our walls and invade our homes, taking our children captive while we were spiritually asleep. We repent on behalf of the Church of America that in the last Presidential election *[1996]*, nearly fifty percent of registered Christians didn't even trouble themselves enough to vote. Help them to realize what You say in Psalm 12:8.

"The wicked freely strut about when what is vile is honored among men."

52

We repent of our lethargy which has allowed the same conditions to prevail as in Isaiah's day which produced a dearth of heroes, warriors, judges, prophets, elders, captains, men of rank, counselors and skilled craftsmen.

"I will make boys their officials; mere children will govern them."
Isaiah 3:4

Lord, bring back to America Godly statesmanship.

We repent of the lust of the flesh, the lust of the eyes and the pride of life, our haughty attitudes and arrogant ways. Forgive us, Lord, for the Church resembling so much the world that our children can't tell the difference. Forgive us, Lord, for being so conditioned by the media that we have lost the ability to blush (Jeremiah 3:3).

On behalf of the Church of the Lord Jesus Christ, we repent of half-heartedness. Lord, forgive the Church in America for breathing in the anesthesia of the spirit of this age and lapsing into a state of spiritual stupor and being mesmerized by anemic religion and becoming complacent. Forgive us for our apathy toward the things of God. Forgive us for not seeking You with our whole heart, mind and strength.

We repent of allowing our spiritual muscles to atrophy. We repent of lapsing into a spiritually vegetative state while a battle rages over our head. Forgive us for our naivete and ignorance of the warfare that is ripping us off and taking captive our children.

We humble ourselves, confess and repent, Lord, that we have set up idols in Your house--idols of silver and gold made by hands of men. They have mouths but cannot speak. There are no utterances except by Your Spirit. They have eyes but cannot see. We have become ignorant and naïve and lacked discernment and spiritual perception. Give us Your vision. They have hands but cannot feel. We have been rendered impotent and useless to do anything with human hands. Without Your Spirit, we are helpless. They have feet but cannot walk. We go nowhere except we are carried along by the Spirit of the Lord (Psalm 115:4-7). Otherwise, all activity becomes an exercise in futility. For this, Lord, we repent, and ask forgiveness. Thank You for hearing our prayers of repentance.

In Jesus' name, amen.

~ 15 ~

REMOVAL OF
REPROACH
FROM THE CHURCH

⚘

Dear Lord, we find ourselves in a weakened condition resembling the seven sons of Sceva. The enemy has come and stated: "Jesus I know, Paul I know about, but who are you," and many Christians have found themselves running out of the house beaten and wounded (Acts 19:14-16). In many cases, we have become a laughingstock, a hissing, a byword, a conversation piece to be bantered about by society and a reproach to You and the glorious Body of Christ. For this we repent and ask forgiveness.

We're weary of the Church being ripped off, being brought to their knees, bowing before an inferior evil power and brought to an early demise. Remove the reproach from Your Church. We cry out to You this day. You are our only hope.

"As the eyes of slaves look to the hand of their master, as the eyes of a maid look to the hand of her mistress, so our eyes look to the Lord our God, till he shows us his mercy."

Psalm 123:2

"Have mercy on us, O Lord, have mercy on us, for we have endured much contempt. We have endured much ridicule from the proud, much contempt from the arrogant."

Psalm 123:3, 4

Let not the world say, "Where is Your God?" but let the Church be able to say to them, "Here is Your God."

"See, the Sovereign Lord comes with power, and his arm rules for him. . . ."

Isaiah 40:10

Lord, we refuse to settle for man's idea of church with its traditions, Madison Avenue and flesh. Restore Your Church and once again visit Your assembly with such love and power of God that the reproach can be removed and once again Your Body can be respected, honored, and highly revered by saint and sinner.

"Let the priests, who minister before the Lord, weep between the temple porch and the altar. Let them say, 'Spare your people, O Lord, do not make your inheritance an object of scorn, a byword among the nations. Why should they say among the peoples, Where is their God?'"

Joel 2:17

~~~~~
**"Let our children no longer chuckle at a first-rate power that is being held hostage by a second-rate power."**
~~~~~

Help the Church to realize that either they stay so up-to-date with You and continually say, "Where is the Lord, what is He doing?" or if they don't, the world will look at us and say, "Where is Your God?"

Visit us Lord with Your power, Your might and a fresh anointing. Bring back Your glory to Your Church so the reproach can be wiped away. Let our children no longer chuckle at a first-rate power that is being held hostage by a second-rate power. We claim Your Word in Isaiah 54:4.

"Do not be afraid; you will not suffer shame. Do not fear disgrace; you will not be humiliated. You will forget the shame of your youth and remember no more the reproach of your widowhood."

Hasten the day, Dear Lord, and thank You for hearing our prayer.

In Jesus' name, amen.

~ 16 ~

CONDUCTING SPIRITUAL WARFARE IN THE CHURCH

&

Dear Lord, forgive us for prayerlessness which has allowed a second-rate, weaker power to run roughshod over a first-rate power--the Church of the Lord Jesus Christ. As it says in Deuteronomy 32:30, how could one (of the enemy) chase a thousand (of God's people), or two (of the enemy) put ten thousand (of God's people) to flight, **". . .unless their Rock had sold them, unless the Lord had given them up?"**

We pray that the Church would do what it says in Isaiah 52:2.

"Shake off your dust; rise up, sit enthroned, . . .free yourself from the chains on your neck, . . ."

We ask You, Lord, to call together and anoint the intercessors to such an extent that the balance of power would shift in the heavenlies, and we would be the ones, not our enemies, that it would be said that one of us put to flight a thousand; two of us ten thousand; three, one hundred thousand; four, one million; and just seven would route a billion demon spirits.

~~~~~

"Raise up a compassionate, loving, militant Church that will once again be respected in our society and by our adversary."

~~~~~

Once again, Lord, place the scepter firmly back into our hands. Turn a wimpy, anemic, impotent Body of believers into a loving, compassionate, tender, fierce, militant spiritual fighting machine which will serve notice on the powers of darkness and plunder the camp of the enemy. Once again, let us see clearly that God is in her citadels and You have shown Yourself to be her fortress (Psalm 48:3). Then when the diabolical kings and the territorial spirits join forces and advance together, they will see with their own eyes a glorious, vibrant, dynamic, powerful Church of the Lord Jesus Christ and the adversary will be astounded, be seized with trembling and flee in terror (Psalm 48:4-6).

Remind us that ". . .from the days of John the Baptist until now the kingdom of heaven suffereth violence, and the violent take it by force (Matthew 11:12 KJV). Raise up a compassionate, loving, militant Church that will once again be respected in our society and by our adversary. Thank You that "When a man's ways please the Lord, he maketh even his enemies to be at peace with him" (Proverbs 16:7 KJV).

Help us to realize the seriousness of entering into warfare against the arch enemy of our souls and the consequences of being derelict in our responsibility.

60

"A curse on him who is lax in doing the Lord's work! A curse on him who keeps his sword from bloodshed!"

Jeremiah 48:10

We thank You for the balance in Your Word of warfare and love as spoken of in Psalm 144:1, 2.

Praise be to the Lord, my rock, who trains my hands for war, my fingers for battle. He is my loving God. . . ."

Thank You for hearing our prayer.

In Jesus' name, amen.

~ 17 ~

WORSHIP
IN THE CHURCH

☙

Lord, we acknowledge that You are the pre-eminent One. You are all powerful, omnipotent, omniscient and You are omnipresent. There is none other. There is no other God like You. You are superior to every other principality and power and potentate.

Dear Lord, we worship You. We adore You. You are worthy of all our praise. We extol You and exalt You to a high place. Be honored this day and we ask You to turn us into worshippers. Replace grumbling, murmuring, complaining, accusation and heaviness with a garment of praise. Let a mantle of worship descend on us today which will minister to You, bring You great joy, and at the same time, contribute to the revolutionizing of our lives, changing our mindset, turning our captivity, restoring our fortunes and bringing restoration. If we're known for anything, let us be known as lavish worshippers of our Lord and Savior, Jesus Christ.

Motivate us, Lord, to praise and worship You and to pray as never before. As we praise You, Lord, let us see the Church once again, beautiful in its loftiness, the joy of the whole earth, like the utmost heights of Zaphon, the city of the Great King (Psalm 48:2).

We humbly confess this morning, dear Lord, that for so long, we have been self-centered and have even gone to church primarily to be ministered to instead of going to minister unto You. Just as the Son of the living God said He came not to be ministered unto, but to minister and give His life a ransom for many, so re-arrange our mindset and attitude and give us the same heart to first of all, minister unto You, then to Your people. Just like Abraham who left a trail of altars everywhere He went, and it was said of him that he staggered not because he gave glory to God, so give us the heart of a worshipper and we shall not stagger nor stumble (Romans 4:20).

We beseech You, dear Lord, to raise up at this significant hour of history, a worshipping Church. Teach us what it means to move in praise, then into high praise, then enter into the Holy of Holies in a dimension of worship that we have hardly experienced yet.

This day, let the joy of the Lord be our strength. In the midst of our prison, just like Paul and Silas, we will praise You with all of our heart. We will praise You 'til You send an earthquake into our situation and the foundations of our prison are shaken, the prison doors fly open and the chains come loose from everyone in our house. We believe, then, that an anointing for evangelism will come and we claim Acts 16 "household salvation."

In the name of Jesus, amen.

~ 18 ~

YOUTH
IN THE CHURCH

⳽

Dear Lord, we pray that the young generation will not chuckle at the Church nor look at it in a condescending, disrespectful, patronizing manner, but that we could show them the majesty, splendor, integrity, honor and magnificence of Your Body, full of Your Holy presence.

Therefore, Lord Jesus, we pray that the alarm would be sounded on Your Holy hill. We ask You to hasten the day that the glory of the latter house is greater than the former (Haggai 2:9).   Instead of showing our children something which is lukewarm, routine, religious and perfunctory, breathe a fresh breath into Your Church so that we can show them a glorious house, a magnificent edifice made up of all Your called out ones.

Let our children, most of whom have never witnessed the dynamics of Your Spirit brooding over Your people like they did in the Early Awakenings, who have never witnessed the Church in the book of Acts reincarnated, let this generation not just see the triviality, flippancy, shallowness, "Barnum and Bailey" atmosphere and the hype, but let them witness with their own eyes the supremacy, superiority, grandeur, splendor

65

and the magnificence of the Shekinah Glory of God descending upon Your Church.

Instead of them witnessing predictable, boring, mundane religious meetings, let them witness first-hand the awesome, spontaneous, wind of Your Holy Spirit once again blowing through our assemblies to the extent they would hardly know when the meeting began or ended, but they would know that they have personally witnessed the hand of the living God moving among Your people. Let their hearts be indelibly impacted and their minds engraved with glorious images and impressions after having witnessed a Church that resembles the one in the New Testament.

What a landmark experience it would be if our kids could witness with their own eyes a demonstration of the glorious New Testament Church of the Lord Jesus Christ in action. Let it be as stated in Psalm 48:12, 13.

"Walk about Zion, go around her, count her towers, consider well her ramparts, view her citadels, that you may tell of them to the next generation."

In Jesus' name, amen.

~ 19 ~

RESTORATION OF ZEAL TO THE CHURCH

CR

Forgive us, Lord, for losing our first love. Do not spew us out of Your mouth. Give us more time. Stir the embers which are barely glowing which are about to smoke and be extinguished and re-ignite in us a passion for the Lord Jesus Christ as we have never known in our entire lifetime. Help us to realize that the only thing that is going to accomplish the purposes of God in our life, in this city, and in this nation is the zeal of the Lord of Hosts (Isaiah 9:7).

We want our hearts to burn within us as the disciples' hearts did on the road to Emmaus after You broke bread with them and their eyes were opened. Open our eyes. Indelibly burn in our hearts the vision of the Lord Jesus Christ for a glorious Church on this earth before You return again. Help us to fully occupy 'til then. We ask You, Lord, to so stir up the Church in Atlanta that we would rise up from our lackadaisical attitude and seek You with an unbridled passion. We pray that You would do such a work in the businessmen of this city that they would seek after You as if they were seeking after silver and gold.

Lord, we beseech You, on behalf of the Church of the Lord Jesus Christ, breathe on us the breath of the living God. Energize us, recommission us, re-ignite our cold, indifferent, stony hearts. Bring back the devotion, the commitment, the fervor, the fire, the passion for Jesus and Your zeal. Give us a spiritual spine of steel. Help us to take a stand when all others crumple. Bring back old-fashioned resolve to press in to You to seek Your face.

Let it be said of us as it was said of You when You cleansed the temple, **". . .Zeal for your house will consume me" (John 2:17).** Let it be that the zeal of the Lord will consume us and let that be the only thing that consumes us. Jesus Christ is the only consumption we will ever experience. Help us to receive Your challenge this day to be men and women of prayer and the Word and men and women of faith. As a matter of fact, let that be our greatest ambition in life, to fulfill Your total calling for us and never to make peace with mediocrity.

By Your grace, we will pay the price. We will be lovers of God more than lovers of pleasure. We will turn away from a creature-comfort mentality. We choose to leave the lap of luxury and the couch of comfort, and by the grace of God, we will become spiritual vigilantes. We pray according to Isaiah 62:1.

"For Zion's sake I will not keep silent, for Jerusalem's sake I will not remain quiet, till her righteousness shines out like the dawn, her salvation like a blazing torch."

In Jesus' name we pray. Amen.

~ 20 ~

THE ANOINTING

CR

Dear Lord, let this prayer count for eternity. We ask You to so anoint our prayer that like Samuel, who was given to the Lord and who was a worshipper, every one of our words in prayer would hit its target and none would fall to the ground.

We acknowledge, Lord, that we cannot improve on Your ministry, nor can we apologize for it. We thank You that You were anointed by the Holy Spirit and power. You went around doing good and healing all who were under the power of the devil because God was with You (Acts 10:38). Give us the same anointing to heal all who are under the clutches of darkness.

Into this dark, depraved society of ours, riddled through and through with satanic activity and demonic personalities, we ask You, Lord, to burst upon the scene of this city with Your resurrection life, with all of its purity, cleanliness, fire, fervor, love, passion, healing and strength. Let that resurrection power ebb and flow through the lives of Your children this day to the extent that they would realize that something Holy and Divine is surging and pulsating through every fiber of their being--spirit, soul and body, and they are personal recipients of a Sovereign visitation of Your anointing.

Help us to be found in such a place of fellowship with You that You would endow us with Your anointing which is like a savor, like perfume which operated like osmosis wherever we go. Whether we say anything or not, it just ministers, and according to scripture, wherever we go, this anointing savor ministers death to demon spirits of death, and at the same time, ministers life, encouragement and edification to everyone we meet who has the Spirit of the life (2 Corinthians 2:16).

Lord, we ask You to hone, intensify and accelerate this anointing in our lives, not for our self-aggrandizement or personal prestige, but for Your glory. We pray that we would be in such intimate fellowship with You, so accurately represent You, be so much the salt of this earth, that everywhere we go, a chain reaction would set into motion simply by virtue of the fact that the man or woman of God has come on the premises, and this anointing would do its sovereign office work.

Lord, we desperately need to be up-to-date with You and be on the cutting edge of what the Spirit is saying and doing. Without vision, the Word says, Your people are perishing. Likewise, for lack of knowledge, Your people are perishing. God help us not to crystallize into some lethargic ecclesiastical stupor. We desperately need a fresh visitation from on high. Lord, rend the heavens and come down. Let the anointing be as fresh as the morning dew. Gives us new wineskins that can contain the new wine, and not like the old wineskins that burst when the Spirit moves and can't hold it.

We repent of our unanointed religious exercises in futility. We repent of quenching the Spirit and extinguishing His fire. We repent of having a form of godliness, but denying the power thereof. We repent of prayerlessness. Lord, we ask You to reduce us back down to the simplicity which is in Christ Jesus and return the Church back to its initial mandate--if it's known for anything, it will be known as a House of Prayer for all nations.

Visit us, Lord, with Your power, Your might and a fresh anointing. Bring back Your glory to Your Church so the reproach can be wiped away. Let our children no longer chuckle at a first-rate power that is being held hostage by a second-rate power. Hasten the day that it will not be commonplace for Your people, who are called by Your name, to fall like flies and be run over roughshod by disease, darkness and death. But once again, let there be a resurgence of might, a demonstration of Your power and deliverance. Let healing power once again flow freely into the walking wounded, the pain-racked bodies and the desperate. By Your anointing, break the bands of wickedness and the death sentence from Your hurting people. Restore health, prosperity and peace.

~~~~~

"No longer will there be cranked-out unanointed messages which give Your people more head knowledge and outlines and do nothing to radically transform lives."

~~~~~

We pray that no longer will there be an ignorance among the majority of Your people concerning what the anointing really is. No longer will we perpetuate fraud among Your people by misrepresenting to Christians and their children a sterile, impotent version of "Americanized" Church which has practically no resemblance to what we read about in New Testament and the book of Acts. No longer will there be cranked-out unanointed messages which give Your people more head knowledge and outlines, and do nothing to radically transform lives. No longer will there be presentations from our pulpits which are nothing more than the letter of the law which kills without the anointing of Your Spirit which gives life. No longer will there be a regimented presentation of scripture verses, outlines and notes without the corresponding quickening to impact the listeners and bring forth much fruit.

We pray for the disconsolate, downcast, oppressed, despairing, those who have had a dark, foreboding cloud of gloom descend upon their lives--darkness so thick that you can nearly touch it. Be the Lily of their Valley, the Bright and Morning Star.

Bring the anointing spoken of in Isaiah 61 that will **". . .comfort all who mourn, and provide for those who grieve in Zion, to bestow on them a crown of beauty, instead of ashes, the oil of gladness instead of mourning, and a garment of praise instead of a spirit of despair"** (Isaiah 61:2, 3).

Let this anointing be so powerful and residual upon their lives this day that even though they feel exhausted, wasted, weary, tired of fighting, worn from the intensity of the battle, there is a release of resurrection virtue in their lives. Let it be so powerful that at the end of this day they actually feel energized with new hope, vision, strength, vitality, expectancy, enthusiasm and new motivation to "go for it." Let them experience the supernatural joy of the Lord rising within their hearts which is their strength.

Lord, we need You. Unless You do it, it's not going to happen. Unless the Lord builds the house, its builders labor in vain. Unless the Lord watches over the city, the watchmen stand guard in vain. Lord, we desperately need Your anointing which breaks the yoke, releases captives and heals wounds. Thank You, Lord. You indeed are the God of the new beginnings.

We pray that the life of the Lord would flow freely, profusely, unabated, unhindered, like a cascading river of pure water. We pray a fresh anointing in our lives. For those who have lost the lustre, fervor, zest and enthusiasm of fellowshipping with You, we ask You to put them back on the cutting edge of walking in the Spirit and being up-to-date with what You are doing and saying. Help us to be like the children of Issachar who knew what season they were in, had an understanding of their times and knew what to do in that season. We pray Galatians 5:25.

"Since we live by the Spirit, let us keep in step with the Spirit."

We pray now an impartation of supernatural resilience and strength to press in for those who have taken hold of the horns of the altar and are fighting for theirs' or others' lives. Lord, let this not be another perfunctory prayer, but let the unction of heaven be on it. Let the breath of God grace our requests and let the anointing do its office work. Thank You for fresh oil from the throne.

In Jesus' name, amen.

SPIRITUAL AWAKENING

CR

Dear Lord, we desperately need nothing less than a historically unprecedented spiritual visitation which will supersede anything history has ever witnessed. We personally invite You, at whatever the cost, to invade our Americanized, lukewarm, sterile, powerless, unanointed, business as usual, perfunctory church gatherings and come with a life transforming, breath of God, miracle producing, fruit bearing move of Your Holy Spirit. Our hearts are hungry. Help us to leave our comfort zone and pray like it says in Isaiah 62:6, 7.

"I have posted watchmen on your walls, O Jerusalem; they will never be silent day or night. You who call on the Lord, give yourselves no rest, and give him no rest till he establishes Jerusalem and makes her the praise of the earth."

We pray for the Church of the Lord Jesus Christ in Atlanta and America. You love it beyond description. You died for it. It is blood-bought and blood-washed, and we pray today that You would ignite it with spiritual fire. Whatever it costs, we ask You, Lord, to bring a revival of the proportions of and even greater than the First Awakening in 1737, the Second Awakening in 1792, the Third Awakening or Prayer Revival in 1857, the Fourth Awakening in 1904, the Welsh Revival in 1904, the Latter Rain Movement in Canada In 1947, Azusa

Street, and the renewal of the power and anointing and gifts of Your Holy Spirit which began in the 1960's and 1970's.

Lord, prepare our hearts for the visitation of Your Spirit which has been promised in scripture. Like Daniel, when he discovered through the Word that the seventy years of desolation of Jerusalem would come to an end, he didn't just sit back and watch history roll. He entered into fervent, effectual, travailing prayer with all of his heart to pray in the purposes, times and seasons of the Lord. So, Lord, help us by Your Spirit to do likewise (Daniel 9:1-20).

~~~~~

"Lord, help us to be like the children of Issachar, who knew the season they were in and knew what to do in that season."

~~~~~

It's obvious, Lord, You are shaking all things just as much in the spiritual as in the natural. It's beginning to become clear it will no longer be business as usual. You are bursting on the scene of our lives to upset the status quo. We desperately need to be up-to-date with You, to be on the cutting edge of what the Spirit is saying and doing. Without vision Your people perish (Proverbs 29:18). God, help us not to crystallize into some lethargic ecclesiastical stupor. We desperately need a fresh visitation from on high. Rend the heavens and come down.

Lord, help us to be like the children of Issachar, who knew the season they were in and knew what to do in that season. Help us not to be like those in Luke 19 who did not recognize the day of Your visitation and consequently destructive forces came upon their city; it was left desolate.

We pray for those so-called nominal Christians, who don't have a clue as to what time it is historically, are oblivious to what the Lord is doing or what the Spirit is saying, who are vegetating in their pews as if having had a frontal lobotomy, slouched in their pews, singing the first, second, and last. God have mercy upon the American Church, that we would wake up from our slumber, leave dead gatherings which have a form of godliness but deny the power thereof, forsake man's traditions and methods and get with Your program. Turn us into new wineskins which will be able to contain the new wine of Your Spirit and not burst when You pour it out. Pre-empt our man-made agendas with Your agenda.

Lord, motivate us to rise up from our beds of ease, laps of luxury and couches of comfort, to rouse ourselves, hear Your trumpet blast, clothe ourselves with Your strength, put on Your garments of splendor, arise and sit enthroned (Isaiah 52:2). We ask You, Lord, to raise up an army of intercessors to stand in the gap and make up the hedge for our city and America. The effectual, fervent prayer of a righteous person avails much. Raise up the righteous and put down the wicked.

We cry out to You, Lord God of Israel, Who slumbers not nor do You sleep. Hear our voice. Respond to our prayers in such a historic way that neither we, nor this city, nor this nation, will ever be the same. Shake us to the core of the depths of our mortal being. Respond to our prayers as You did to David's in Psalm 18. Tremble the earth. Shake the foundations of the mountains. Let smoke arise from Your nostrils, consuming fire from Your mouth. Part the heavens. Come down. Mount the cherubim. Go for it. Move out on the wings of the wind. Advance with hailstones and bolts of lightning out of the brightness of Your presence. Thunder from heaven. Cause Your voice to resound. Let it reverberate throughout the corridors of this city. Let this entire area feel the hot blast of Your breath. Move in such a sovereign way that it will be noised here and abroad that Jesus Christ is Lord over our city and nation. Shoot Your arrows, scatter the enemy, send great bolts of lightning, rout them, shake the foundations of this city until they are laid bare (Psalm 18:14, 15). Reach down from on high, take hold of us, draw us out of deep waters, rescue us from our powerful enemy, from our foes who are too strong for us (Psalm 18:16, 17).

Be our support, our bulwark, our strong foundation, our stay, our rear guard, our fortress. Bring us into a spacious place by great deliverance. You've done it before and we know You're preparing to do it again, even with greater magnitude than history has ever witnessed. Prepare us, Lord, for the greatest revival of all times which will counter the intense darkness that will be unleashed by the wicked one. We can't wait to see great conviction, repentant weeping, radically changed lives and a society impacted by a supernatural, God-breathed revival. We hunger to see Your glory brought back into Your Church to replace that which is trivial, perfunctory, predictable and boring. We cry out as David did in Psalm 63:1, 2 and give us this same hunger.

"O God, you are my God, earnestly I seek you; my soul thirsts for you, my body longs for you, in a dry and weary land where there is no water. I have seen you in the sanctuary and beheld your power and your glory."

Lord, we pray that there would be launched the greatest New Testament evangelism that this city has ever known. Let it go beyond the mere handing out of tracts which some sneer at and throw on the ground. We pray a sovereign move of Your Spirit because of such intense concerts of prayer which will result in people falling on their faces before Almighty God under deep, intense, piercing conviction. Let it be that they experience deep sorrow for their sins and for having grieved the Spirit of the Lord as they are marvelously converted and translated from the kingdom of darkness into the kingdom of Your dear Son.

If it happened in previous God-breathed revivals, it can happen again on an even greater scale because Your Word promises us that there is going to be a visitation of Your Spirit to upset the dismal status quo in the anemic American Church. You said the glory of the latter house would greatly exceed that of the former (Haggai 2:9). We thank You, Lord, that a day is coming that the knowledge of the glory of the Lord will cover the earth like the waters cover the sea (Isaiah 11:9), and You have saved the best wine 'til last (John 2:10). What better time to ignite these revival fires than now. Lord, hasten the day.

We appropriate Your Word in Isaiah 64:1-5 for the days ahead.

"Oh, that you would rend the heavens and come down, that the mountains would tremble before you! As when fire sets twigs ablaze and causes water to boil, come down to make your name known to your enemies and cause the nations to quake before you! . . .you did awesome things that we did not expect, . . .Since ancient times no one has heard, no ear has perceived, no eye has seen any God besides you, who acts on behalf of those who wait for him. You come to the help of those who gladly do right. . . ."

Forgive us, Lord, for becoming so secular, materialistic and arrogant, so self sufficient, so independent, so sophisticated, that we don't even call on Your name. Raise up intercessors. Come down and tabernacle among us. Let us sense Your awesome, manifest presence. Bring a spiritual awakening that will impact every area of our lives, and once again, as in the days of old, let us see the healing power of the Lord released in our midst.

We ask You, Lord, to bring a burden of intercession to the American Church and to the Body of Christ in this city. We know that before every historic awakening, there was a revival of prayer. Jolt us to rise up from our sedentary lifestyles, "smell the coffee", shake ourselves from our American complacency so we can take our places as watchmen and watchwomen on the wall. Give us the spiritual fortitude to stand in the gap, make up the hedge, weep between the altar and the porch, take hold of the horns of the altar and conduct kingdom business in prayer. Give us the grace and perseverance to take a prayer assignment and relentlessly, through intercession, wrestle with dark powers, enforce the victory that was won at Calvary and take it all the way to the gates. Let us become so notorious in prayer that we will come together one evening as an intercessory, executive body, decree a thing in prayer agreement and read about the results in the next morning's headlines.

Lord, our young people need to witness what happened in the days of David Edwards, George Finney and George Whitfield. They need to witness, firsthand, hardhearted, stonecold, indifferent, depraved, wicked men and women stumbling into our services and as soon as they cross the threshold, because the meetings have been soaked in prayer and the presence of the Lord is so profuse, they come under strong, piercing, intense conviction, begin to weep, cry out to God for mercy and forgiveness, fall on their knees in repentance and come up marvelously, radically saved. Our children have never witnessed this in their lifetime. Lord, it's time that they see it. Whatever the cost, raise up intercessors and bring a revival of this proportion that will sweep our city and nation.

~~~~~

"Forgive us, Lord, for becoming so secular, materialistic and arrogant, that we don't even call on Your name."

~~~~~

We thank You that it's already begun, and we have hardly seen anything yet compared to what's preparing to happen. We thank You, Lord, that because of fervent prayers that avail much, You're about to do a thing that will cause both ears of everyone who hears about it to tingle.

Lord, we use the same terminology as used in scripture and pray in the beginnings of a revival of historic proportions. We pray in an "outpouring of the Spirit" (Like rain or fire falling, or wind blowing), "The renewing of God's mighty deeds" as spoken of in Habakkuk 3:2. We pray in "the glory of the Lord returning to Your temple," "God healing our land," and "the time of God's visitation" with Your manifest presence.

Lord, we'd love to drive down the highways of our city and see cars by the hundreds pulled over, people bent over their steering wheels weeping uncontrollably under the strong, convicting power of the Holy Spirit as their hearts are melted, they repent and turn wholeheartedly to You. We'd love to experience what they experienced in Finney's day, that there was such a volume of prayer that territorial spirits and principalities and powers were pulled down, and the incredible, awesome power of the Holy Spirit so filled that vacuum that there were areas in the city through which people could not pass without being born again. Lord, You've done it before. We believe You're preparing to do it again in answer to our effectual, fervent prayers.

We so hunger for Your presence, Your integrity, Your character, Your magnificence, Your splendor, Your majesty that we now humble ourselves at Your feet to pray prayers to prepare the way of the Lord, so that once again, You can raise up a highway of Holiness and restore glory to Your Church. We earnestly seek You. Our soul thirsts for You. Our body longs for You in a dry and weary land where there is no water. Let the water of life flow freely in our lives and our society. We are going to pray that which is now a trickle move into a stream, then into a river, then into a sea and finally, into a mighty

FROM THE HEART OF AN INTERCESSOR

ocean. Inundate our city and nation with nothing less than the awesome visitation of the Trinity of the Father, Son, and Holy Spirit.

We pray that there would mount up such a movement of prayer agreement and power that You would visit us with a fresh move of Your Spirit which would supersede everything and anything that You have ever done in history. It's harvest time, Lord, and You promised that You would pour out Your Spirit on all flesh (Joel 2:28), and You promised greater things than these, than You, Lord Jesus, did while on this earth, will we do (John 14:12). We are seriously seeking Your face. Let the fire fall. Let the glory of the Lord be ushered back into Your Church and start it, Lord, with us right now.

Come, Lord Jesus. This is the day of restoration that the prophets of old spoke of; this is the day You said You would restore the years where evil insects have eaten and robbed from Your people (Joel 2:25). Let this be the year of Jubilee, a special time in which all of our debts are cancelled, and the prisoners are released from their grueling captivity from under a cruel taskmaster, making bricks without straw.

We want to be part of the solution and not part of the problem. We want to be known as repairers of broken walls, restorers of streets with dwellings, and we ask You, Lord, in these momentous days where You have just begun to pour out the latter rain of Your Spirit, to use us to rebuild ancient ruins and raise up age-old foundations. Give us the spiritual power to dispossess the gates of the enemy and possess the land, to take back that which we have previously lost by default. We thank You, Lord, as we speak, there is a centrifuge of Your Spirit moving in such a manner that before this day is over, many will know that they have been visited by the living Lord Jesus Christ and that God Almighty has intervened in human affairs in a supernatural way.

We believe we are on the verge of an unprecedented outpouring of Your Spirit on the downtown streets of our city. Let these wandering, vagabond, homeless people experience what it means that God is Lord, that You are the One Who made them, that they are Your people and each individual is a sheep of Your pasture. Be a God of destiny to them this day. Pour out Your Spirit on the streets of our great city.

Lord, remove from the Church doctrines of demons which deprive Your people of the power and the anointing and the deliverance. Remove far from us the teaching that these things were only for the days of the apostles. Etch into our spirits what it says in Hebrews that Jesus Christ is the same yesterday, today and forever. Remove from us the teachings of dispensationalism which rob and deprive Your people today of the power and deliverance and miracles which they so desperately need to be overcomers and bring about this revival. Restore Your Church. Lord, bring Your glory and power back into the Body of Christ.

~~~~~
**"Lord, remove from the Church doctrines of demons which deprive Your people of the power and the anointing and the deliverance."**
~~~~~

This is the generation of prayer. Lord, help us to heed the scripture in I Peter 4:7.

"The end of all things is near. Therefore be clear minded and self-controlled so that you can pray."

We realize throughout history that every spiritual awakening has been preceded by a mighty revival of prayer. We thank You, Lord, that history is about to repeat itself. For the last 300 years, we have had a major war in the sixties and a historic revival at the turn of the century and it's about to happen again. As we fervently pray, we're on the threshold of the greatest awakening America has ever known.

We appropriate Your Word in Isaiah 64:1-5 for the days ahead.

"Oh, that you would rend the heavens and come down, that the mountains would tremble before you! As when fire sets twigs ablaze and causes water to boil, come down to make your name known to your enemies and cause the nations to quake before you! . . .you did awesome things that we did not expect. . . .Since ancient times no one has heard, no ear has perceived, no eye has seen any God besides you, who acts on behalf of those who wait for him. You come to the help of those who gladly do right. . . ."

We ask You, Lord, that You would put such a burning passion to once again see You pour out Your Spirit on all flesh, such a hunger and thirst after righteousness. For it is only those who hunger and thirst after righteousness who shall be filled. Grant it that we would set our face like flint, drop our anchor deeply, have great resolve in our heart, burn our bridges behind us, forget the former things, launch into the deep and put our hand to the plow, never looking back, to see the day of Your visitation in our lives in this city and our nation.

In the name of Jesus we pray. Amen.

~ 22 ~

ENCOURAGEMENT

ભ

We praise You, Lord, this day. Morning by morning You hear our voice and morning by morning we lay our requests before You. You have proven Yourself to us over and over again. You have daily loaded us with benefits. You are our Ebenezer--hitherto have You brought us--hitherto You will bring us on. For the disheartened, disconsolate, and those not soon comforted, let them know of a surety that You have not brought them this far to abandon them, but that You are their personal Ebenezer-- hitherto have You brought them--hitherto You will bring them on!

Lord, we stand in the gap for those who desperately need encouragement. Let this be a day in which significant, monumental changes take place in the lives of Your people in this city. For those who are mired down in circumstances and problems which have no human answer, and feel they are on a dead-end road, we pray that they will totally yield themselves and every area of their lives to You. We celebrate You this day as the God of the breakthrough. We celebrate You as the above and beyond God. You are well able to do exceedingly abundantly above all that we ask or think (Ephesians 3:20). Lord, You are well able. By many or by few is of no

85

consequence to You. We speak to the mountains in these peoples' lives to be removed in Jesus' name.

Lord, this city is a dry and thirsty land where there is very little water. We pray for those sojourners who are thirsty, empty and rejected, those who feel as if they have been thrust out into a bitter winter storm, alone and with time and provision about to run out. We intercede for those, who in the lonely hours of the night have wept so many tears, there are no more to weep. We corporately join with intercessors all over this city and ask You to supernaturally pour out Your love, acceptance, approval and compassion. Be the Lover of their souls. Be to them a Father, a Husband, a Provider, a Sustainer, an Encourager, One Who comes alongside. Represent them. Be their Spokesman. Fight their battles and stand in-between them and their personal destroyer. Drive from their lives the accuser of the brethren who is busy accusing all of us before the Father twenty four hours a day.

~~~~~

"We intercede for those, who in the lonely hours of the night have wept so many tears, there are no more to weep."

~~~~~

For the abandoned and lonely, for those who feel as if You have forgotten their name and address, we pray that today, before the midnight hour, they would experience not only Your presence, but Your manifest presence. Banish the loneliness and indescribable pain. Fill in the hollow, empty places. Help them to, not only experience life in Christ, but life more abundantly.

For those who are experiencing stress, personal turmoil, emotional anguish, mental torment; for those who are caught in the crossfire of family or relational conflict; for those who are living in a virtual personal war zone, come Lord Jesus. Rend the heavens and come down. Come as the Prince of Peace. Bring Your supernatural tranquility. Pour in the oil of Your Spirit and speak peace to tempestuous waves.

Now, for those who have been battling deep discouragement, disappointment and oppression, we say to them, "It's not too late. You who are distraught and weeping internally, you feel like your heart is about to break open, it's not too late. The Lord is never too late. His grace is still extended. His hand of mercy is still open. His arm is not too short, nor His ears dull to hear (Isaiah 59:1). There is still time. He can intervene, if necessary, supernaturally. It's not too late."

For those who feel like their chariot wheels have come off, be the Great Expediter, the Heavenly Facilitator. Just like the iron gate opened of its own accord when the angel delivered Peter out of prison, so send forth angels to open the iron gate that looms large over the lives of Your people. Let faith surge in their hearts to the extent that they could speak to the mountains in their lives--not by might nor power, but by Your Spirit--this mountain, too, shall be removed (Mark 11:23).

We pray for those who feel as if life has left them behind, and the adverse one has whispered in their ear that it's all over, they are beyond their prime, they're over the hill, lost opportunities have left them in the dust, they are full of regret and are going through life looking through the rearview mirror. We ask You, Lord, to gently arrest them. Defuse the misinformation of darkness. Deal with the delusion and lies of the enemy of their souls and help them to rejoice in whatever age they are. Help them to realize, as Paul acknowledged, that at the appointed time they were born and at the appointed time You will usher them into that arena of their lives for which You have been preparing them all these years. Reaffirm to them You are a God of times and seasons.

We intercede for, stand in the gap and make up the hedge for, those who are suffering from paralysis, the paralysis of deep, excruciatingly painful depression. We pray for those who are under such a spell of darkness and are momentarily out of commission. Lord, minister to those who feel like they have been drained. Something has entered their life which has immobilized them like an anesthesia of the adversary himself and they are despairing of themselves, their future, their abilities and life itself.

We speak this Word right into the face of the enemy himself who is haranguing and tormenting Your people about the days to come.

"'For I know the plans I have for you,' declares the Lord, 'plans to prosper you and not to harm you, plans to give you hope and a future. Then you will call upon me and come and pray to me, and I will listen to you. You will seek me and find me when you seek me with all your heart.'"

Jeremiah 29:11-13

Lift Your people out of the slough of despondency. Shake them to the core of their being. Awaken them to the incredible potential they have in the Lord and breathe upon them a fresh breath of God. Be an oxygen line to them while they are under stress, to minister Divine CPR and rejuvenate them.

For those who are suffering depression, break off these people a heavy, dark foreboding cloud. We pray for them Your Word in Psalm 51:12, 13.

"Restore to me the joy of your salvation and grant me a willing spirit, to sustain me. Then I will teach transgressors your ways, and sinners will turn back to you."

Let the joy of the Lord be their strength. Converge on them, dear Lord, suddenly, meet them right where they are.

Instead of entertaining self-pity, licking their wounds, and feeling sorry for themselves, all of a sudden they will find themselves being restored, the joy of the Lord being their strength, and they will begin to minister to the Lord, reach out to others and teach transgressors Your ways. Do it today, Lord. It is going to be revolutionary.

You foul spirits of dark, foreboding, oppressive depression and suicide, you know exactly who we're talking about. The light of the Lord exposes you. Right now, in a concert of prayer agreement, let the glorious, brilliant, luminescent light of our Lord and Savior, Jesus Christ, pierce through the darkness and bring supernatural hope. With New Testament authority which has been vested in us, and as we are corporately turned into an executive body of prayer, we bind the diabolical entities that are running roughshod over God's people as if it were open season on Christians and trying to capitalize upon their circumstances.

~~~~~

"Remove the poison-tipped arrows, the fiery darts, the evil venom which resides in hateful, vindictive words."

~~~~~

Listen up, you spirit forces of darkness. You may have come this far, but you're not coming any further. Just as the Lord Jesus Christ commissioned the disciples in Luke 10 to rend and trample on snakes and scorpions and to overcome all the power of the enemy with the promise that nothing would harm them, and as he said, "so send I you," with the same authority, we do likewise. We declare the superiority and Lordship of Jesus Christ over their lives.

We ask You, Lord, to personally deal with the tormentor who is making the lives of Your people miserable day and night. Drive out the one who has been holding them hostage and making their lives not worth living. We celebrate You this morning as the One Who paid the supreme price for us to bring us, not only life, but life more abundantly. We join with prayer warriors all over this city. Reach into the lives that are not worth living, the ones who have momentarily entertained death wishes and opened the door for the death angel. Drive out from their presence the grim reaper and rush into their lives with resurrection life, light, power, strength, encouragement and edification. Let faith rise in their hearts as never before.

Remove the poison tipped arrows, the fiery darts, the evil venom which resides in hateful, vindictive words. Cleanse their entire system, spirit, soul and body, by the precious Blood of Jesus Christ and the washing of the Word. Let them feel the cleansing agent of the Blood of Christ flowing through every area of their life. Let the results of this divine transaction be evident this very day.

Now, in Jesus' name, for those who have been loosed from the heavy, dark power of depression, oppression and suicide, shower upon them the joy of the Lord. Restore to them the joy of Your salvation so they can be put back into commission and teach transgressors Your ways. Remove the cobwebs from their brain. Dispel doubt and unbelief. Let faith loom large in their life. Re-orient them to begin thinking once again Your thoughts. Lord, we ask You to give them Your perspective concerning themselves and their future. Let them begin to speak what the Word says about them. Remove confusion and give them the mind of Christ.

We thank You, Lord, there is no sin too big, no pit too deep, no stumbling too severe that You can't forgive. Your Blood covers it all. Therefore, we defuse the lies of darkness, intercept his deception and his misinformation. We neutralize the enemy's malignant, insidious work, and cause to cease and desist his tormenting deception. We pray to loose the bands of wickedness around the minds of Your people and let them go. Let them experience a degree of freedom like they have never known before. Be to them a Sovereign Deliverer.

Thank You for the Holy Spirit Whose other name is Comforter, and that You sent Him that we should not be orphans. We ask You for such a rich anointing to flow, that the downtrodden, lonely, discouraged and rejected will experience You as their Comforter, and they would no longer feel or act like an orphan. Be to them at this moment a personal Heavenly Father. Let the warmth of Your love flow profusely and lavishly through every area of their life.

We thank You, Lord, when the enemy comes in like a flood, You will raise up a standard against him. Thank You, Lord, as we fervently pray, we believe the answer is on the way. To the downcast and downtrodden, we ask You this day, to come as the lifter of their heads.

We ask You, Lord, to open their eyes, just as Elisha prayed to open the eyes of his servant who was terrified when he saw they were surrounded by an evil army that was far superior and vastly outnumbered them. It appeared as if it was only a matter of time. Sure, sudden destruction appeared to be imminent and as Elisha prayed, and You opened his eyes, all of a sudden, to his amazement, he saw an awesome army of angels which caused the enemy forces to pale into insignificance in comparison (2 Kings 6). Open the eyes of Your people. Let them know there is another dimension out there which cannot be seen with their human eyes. Cause to rush into the void of their lives, angels, strong warring angels with fiery, double-edged swords. Also, bring in ministering angels, like the ones who came to Jesus after the severe testing in the wilderness.

We ask You to strike supernatural hope and encouragement into the hearts of Your saints. Lift them out of their shriveled up view of the future. Give them Your outlook, Your attitude and Your perspective. Let them smell the smoke of victory in the camp. Impart to them Godly gusto. Whatever is going on in the heavenlies because of their faithful prayers over a long period of time, let that great reservoir in heaven which contains prayers mixed with incense suddenly come cascading down onto earth in some tangible, concrete form--in the form of healing, finances, reconciliation of relationships, or the salvation of a lost loved one.

Give them such a spirit of conquest like Joshua in his latter years, that all they would have to do is look at a mountain, seeing an opportunity, and say, "I'll take it. Give me that mountain." Give them such a mind set of conquest that they will say as Daniel said in Daniel 11:32 that the people that know their God shall be strong, and do exploits.

~~~~~

"Lord, we don't want to just be in an existence mode or just have a survival mentality."

~~~~~

Let this year go down in their personal history as an unprecedented year of great exploits.

Lord, we don't want to just be in an existence mode or just have a survival mentality. We want to experience what You meant when You said that You not only bring life but bring it more abundantly. We want to draw deeply from the wells of salvation. Let it be that out of our innermost beings will flow rivers of living water and we say to this reservoir, "Spring up, O well."

92

Restore the joy of our salvation. Let the same joy that sustained You, Lord, on Your way to the cross, sustain Your children this day. Help us to fix our eyes on Jesus, the Author and Perfecter of our faith, Who for the joy that was set before You, endured the cross, scorned the shame, and sat down at the right hand of the throne of God (Hebrews 12:2).

Make known to them the path of life. Fill them with joy in Your presence. Thank You, Lord, that Your anger lasts only a moment, but Your favor lasts a lifetime. Thank You that though weeping may remain for a night, rejoicing comes in the morning. Thank You, Lord, for the promise that those who sow in tears will reap with songs of joy, and those who go forth weeping, bearing precious seed, shall doubtless come again with rejoicing, bringing their sheaves with them (Psalm 126:6). Help Your people, with joy, draw water from the wells of salvation (Isaiah 12:2).

Lord, change us into Your same image. We thank You for the scripture in Philippians 1:6 that says,

"being confident of this, that he who began a good work in you will carry it to completion until the day of Christ Jesus."

Let that Word replace the thoughts that come from the whisperer and naysayers. Clear the cobwebs out of our mind. This day, give us the mind of Christ.

To the desperate, give a token of Your love, a token evidence this day that You have not forgotten their address, that their names are etched in the palm of Your hand, that they are not alone in this struggle, and that in answer to their prayers, You are preparing to dispatch angelic emissaries into the battle on their behalf. The angel of the Lord encamps about those who fear Him. We ask You to personally visit those in this city who have not bowed the knee to Baal. Help them to know that it will not always be this way, that You are a

God of times and seasons and that as they seek Your face, help is on the way and healing is waiting in the wings.

May the zeal of the Lord of hosts consume us this day and let that be the only consumption that touches our lives. As we worship You, place a garland of grace about our necks. Energize Your people with resurrection power. Lift up the hands that hang down, confirm feeble knees, make straight paths for our feet, so that which is lame shall not be turned out of the way, but rather healed (Hebrews 12:12, 13).

Right now, in Jesus' name, banish despair and hopelessness and strike hope in the hearts of Your people as never before. Let love, patience, forbearance, gentleness, caring, tenderness--all the attributes of Your Spirit, be theirs. Let this be a time of healing, restoration and reconciliation. Bring encouragement and edification. Enlarge our vision. Impart to us Your joyful anticipation and expectation for what You're preparing to do in the future and the move of God's Spirit which is imminent.

We pray this morning that everyone hearing this prayer, before the day is over, would be lifted out of their slough of despondency, that You would come and break the evil yoke, put to flight the evil oppression, and visit upon Your people with Your awesome presence, love and power. Before the midnight hour, let them know there is a God in Israel, there is a God in the United States of America and there is a God that intervenes in the affairs of man and in their personal life, Who hasn't forgotten their address, Who cares intensely about every minute detail of their lives.

We claim Your Word in Psalm 30:5.

"For his anger lasts only a moment, but his favor lasts a lifetime; weeping may remain for a night, but rejoicing comes in the morning."

Come, Lord Jesus. Be so personal and intimate with Your people. Dry their tears. Be the lifter of their heads. Take them in Your arms. Embrace them. Let them know they are accepted in the Beloved and that You love them unconditionally. Assure them right now that You will never leave them nor forsake them. Let there be such a presence of the Lord that they will know this day is their last lonely, lonesome day.

Encourage Your people that help is on the way. We appropriate this Word for them from Isaiah 42:16.

"I will lead the blind by ways they have not known, along unfamiliar paths I will guide them; I will turn the darkness into light before them and make the rough places smooth. These are the things I will do; I will not forsake them."

Thank You, Lord, that all who are weary and burdened can come to You and You will give them rest. We take Your yoke upon us to learn of You, knowing You are gentle and humble in heart and we find rest for our souls. Your yoke is easy. Your burden is light (Matthew 11:28-29). Thank You for being the lifter of our heads this day.

In Jesus' name we pray. Amen.

FLESH VS. SPIRIT

ଔ

Dear Lord, let Your way be prepared so that these few minutes will hit the mark. Make us efficiency experts in the realm of the Spirit. Let there not be a trace of religion in our prayers. Let us not play religious games ever again nor get involved in ecclesiastical exercises in futility. Move us from religion to relationship.

We ask You to give us, the Body of Christ, a clear distinction between that which is flesh (which profits nothing), and that which is of Your Spirit (which accomplishes everything). Help us not to get involved in anything except it has been bathed in prayer and is birthed by the Spirit of God. We acknowledge Your Word in 1 John 5:4 that whatsoever (not just whosoever, but whatsoever) is born of God overcomes the world. . . We cannot afford to get involved in anything which is not born of God. We're weary of propping up, promoting, hyping and striving in things which are religious, yet don't have Your signature on them.

We confess to You, Lord, that just as the children of Israel diluted the wine with water, so have we. Our silver has become dross. Thoroughly purge away the dross. Remove the impurities. Siphon off the water from the wine of Your Spirit.

Purify it so once again we can experience the pungency, New Testament dynamics and resurrection power.

We ask You to help us to separate the precious from the vile and to make a distinction between the holy and unholy, to utter worthy, not worthless words and so be Your spokesman.

Lord, instruct us in Your ways and Your methods. Your Word says that the children of Israel knew Your acts and Moses knew Your ways. Lord, we not only want to know Your acts, we want to know You, personally, intimately, and unlearn the ways of religion which is riddled through and through with flesh and the carnal Babylonian strategies of this world system. Reduce us back down to the simplicity which is in Christ Jesus. Like Samuel, let none of our words drop to the ground.

Give us keen discernment. We ask You to desensitize us to the voices and influences of this world and sensitize us to the voice of Your Holy Spirit. Spare us from spirits of seduction and conspiracies of enticement as we walk through the landmine of life. We pray, right now, that You would bring into all of our lives deep, piercing conviction of anything we're doing, involved in, or any relationship which is not of Your Spirit.

We can't afford to get involved in anything which does not have built into it Your overcoming power. Lord, help us. There are a lot of drawing cards, a lot of people pulling on us, a lot of calls, a lot of invitations. The only thing we want to get involved in, or give ourselves and anointing to, is that which is birthed of God, which overcomes the world. We thank You as we speak, that You are changing minds and priorities.

Teach us, Lord, to be led by Your Spirit and to operate in the Spirit instead of the flesh. Forgive us for striving and pushing and leveraging and maneuvering and compelling. Teach us to allow the Prince of Peace to do Your work through us so that things can spontaneously fall into place. Teach us to wait upon the Lord. We invite Your Holy Spirit to expedite and facilitate every job and responsibility we have. Holy Spirit, flow through us. We refuse to lean on the arm of flesh, but totally lean on You this day.

We ask You, Lord to rearrange our lives, adjust our priorities, show us what's important in Your eyes and redirect our lives in getting involved in things that have eternal value. Show us where we are in history. Give us a sense of urgency concerning things which are of utmost importance to You. We pray that anything we willfully are involved in which has not been birthed of God and does not have Your anointing, we would drop immediately. And the only things we would invest our lives in and spend our precious time on would be those things which indeed are born of the Spirit of God. Confirm to us what we're to get involved in and give our life to.

~~~~~
**"We pray that anything we willfully are involved in which has not been birthed of God and does not have Your anointing, we would drop immediately."**
~~~~~

Lord, we must hear from You. Thank You for Your Word in Psalm 127:1 that says.

"Unless the Lord builds the house, its builders labor in vain. Unless the Lord watches over the city, the watchmen stand guard in vain."

Forgive us, Lord, for doing our own thing in our own strength, under our own steam. Forgive us for our brilliant exercises in futility.

We pray that religious people would forsake their dead, dull, boring, perfunctory religion and cease wasting time in ecclesiastical exercises in futility and come into an intimate, passionate, vital, living relationship with the Lord Jesus Christ. We pray as David did in Psalm 63:1, 2 (AMP).

"O God, You are my God; earnestly will I seek You; my inner self thirsts for You, my flesh longs and is faint for You, in a dry and weary land, where no water is. So I have looked upon You in the sanctuary, to see Your power and Your glory."

We pray, according to the calling on Jeremiah, to root out, tear down, pluck and destroy lifeless religion which has no anointing, and to plant and build Your true Church which flows freely with the power and love of the Lord Jesus Christ (Jeremiah 1:10). Where the Spirit of the Lord is, there is liberty.

Remove far from us any vestige of religion. God spare Your people from the hectic, frenzied, fast-paced activity of empty, sterile, hollow religious activities. Impart to us an unprecedented disdain for anything religious. Let us be able to smell it a mile away and keep our distance. We hunger for that which has the depth, substance, fullness and fragrance of Your Spirit resident in it. We recoil backwards from that which is ecclesiastical and has the sound of tinkling cymbal and sounding brass. We pray that Your people would be able to distinguish between the two and no longer tolerate such a travesty, such misrepresentation, such counterfeiting of the real thing. We realize if we were guilty of this kind of scandalous misrepresentation in the business world, we would be sued.

We realize, Lord, that in scripture, every time, without exception, that resurrection power was released to free a captive or heal a sick person or raise the dead or cleanse a leper or to release miracle working power or exhibit signs and wonders, without exception, a religious spirit would raise up its ugly head in the form of a scribe, Pharisee, Sanhedrin, teacher of the law or high priest. They would be anointed from the other side and would demonically resist the anointing of Your Spirit. As a matter of fact, they were religious spirits that finally crucified the Lord of glory.

Therefore, without hesitation or apology, we ask You, Lord to expose every religious spirit in our churches, whether it operates in a board of deacons or pontificates from the pulpits of this city. Let them recoil backwards in abject horror and trepidation. Let them gasp and be throttled down and be driven into dry places to await the Judgment Day. In the place of this, Lord, we ask You to impart a fresh anointing and release miracle working power into Your Church. Emanate forth with the essence of Your Spirit, accompanied by a sweet fragrance from the Lord. Let not our church organizations any longer be listed in the Yellow Pages under *Country Club*. We pray there would be such a demonstration of Your Spirit that the world system would be drawn to our gatherings and we would once again witness deep, intense, piercing conviction which would cause peoples' hearts to melt and lives to be permanently, radically transformed.

Deliver the Church from a hectic, frenzied, whirlwind, driven pace of religious activities that You never called them to that rob us of precious time that we could be spending with You and our families. Remove from our lives that which drives us, compels us, frenzies us, wastes us, and help us to experience personally what Your Word means in Isaiah 40:30, 31 (KJV).

"Even the youths shall faint and be weary, and the young men shall utterly fall; but they that wait upon the Lord shall renew their strength; they shall mount up with wings as eagles; they shall run, and not be weary; and they shall walk, and not faint."

Help Christians to realize what it says in 2 Corinthians 3:6 (KJV), that **". . .the letter killeth, but the Spirit giveth life,"** and what Paul said in 1 Corinthians 4:20, that **". . .the kingdom**

of God is not a matter of talk but of power," and what he said in 1 Corinthians 1:17.

"For Christit. . .sent me. . . to preach the gospel--not with words of human wisdom, lest the cross of Christ be emptied of its power."

1 Corinthians 2:4
"My message and my preaching were not with wise and persuasive words, but with a demonstration of the Spirit's power."

Lord, we need more than sermons, outlines, charts, notes, seminars and therapy sessions. We need a modern day demonstration of Your power that will leave us breathless, with our mouths open--awestruck, smitten--something that will indelibly impact our lives forever.

It's one thing for the ship to be in the water, but it's something else for the water to get into the ship. Lord, the water of the spirit of this age has gotten into the ship. Purge from our midst humanistic psychology, sensational hype, soulish co-dependent groups, fleshly therapy sessions and worldly counseling. Help us to understand what scripture means. If any one of you is overtaken in a fault, let him who is spiritual restore such a one in a spirit of meekness (Galatians 6:1).

That is the scriptural qualification for counseling, not a degreed person who has not one ounce of anointing. Help us to be truly spiritual so we can be competent to counsel.

We pray for the intellectuals of this world, that after they have drained their brilliant think tanks, after they have expended all of their resources and run out of options, and after they have bankrupted their humanistic ways, that en masse they would turn to You and we would witness a spiritual awakening of historic proportions. Lord, You did it in the Early

Awakening. You did it in the Welsh Revival. You can do it again. We celebrate You this morning and honor You as an above and beyond God, One Who is ". . .well able to do exceedingly abundantly above all that we can ask or think" (Ephesians 3:20). Come, Lord Jesus. Show Yourself powerful to Your people. Reveal Your right arm. Press these battles to the gates and get glory to Yourself.

~~~~~

"Purge from our midst humanistic psychology, sensational hype, soulish co-dependent groups, fleshly therapy sessions and worldly counseling."

~~~~~

Lord, give us, Your Church, the discernment to recognize that which is of the Spirit of God and that which is of flesh. Let it be said of us as it was prophetically spoken concerning Jesus in Isaiah 11:3. He did not judge by the seeing of his eyes, nor the hearing of his ears.

Hone our spiritual radar to be able to look beyond the camouflage, noise, hype, glitter, extravaganza, promotions, distractions and the deception and truly discern that which is of God. Give Your people the spiritual fortitude to sometimes say, "No!"

Deliver us from traditions of men which make the Word of God of no effect. Deliver us from dead, powerless rituals which have absolutely nothing to do with the Spirit of the living God. Deliver us from meetings which are nothing less than a form of godliness denying the power thereof. Deliver us from religious exercises in futility which are close facsimiles of the real thing but they aren't. Deliver us from ecclesiastical gatherings which are perfunctory, routine, boring, dull, anemic, and have no breath of God, no anointing. You never show up. It's just religious people doing their own religious things.

Give us a strong desire to no longer waste our precious time in these spiritual deserts. Let not the Church of the Lord Jesus Christ resemble a country club. Show us distinctly in Your Word the difference between a worldly organization and a spiritual organism--Your Church. We ask You, Lord, to remove the curse which has come on many Christians because, instead of relying on the risen Lord Jesus Christ and His power and His anointing, they have put their trust in man, psychology, psychiatry, therapy sessions, and self-help groups and have depended on flesh for their strength. Consequently, they have become like a bush in the wastelands and dwell in parched places of a spiritual desert (Jeremiah 17:5, 6).

From this day on we are going to put our total confidence in You and be like a tree planted by the water that sends its roots by the stream and does not fear when heat comes. Its leaves are always green. It has no worries in a year of drought and never fails to bear fruit (Jeremiah 17:7, 8). Blessed are the people who forsake the arm of flesh which shall fail them and trust in the living, risen, anointed, Lord Jesus Christ.

"The Spirit gives life; the flesh counts for nothing. The words I have spoken to you are Spirit and they are life."
John 6:63

Bring back Your glory. Let the Church be the Church.

We humble ourselves, confess and repent, Lord, that we have in the past set up idols in Your house--idols of silver and gold made by the hands of men. They have mouths but cannot speak. There are no utterances except by Your Spirit.

They have eyes but cannot see. We have become ignorant and naïve, and lacked discernment and spiritual perception. Give us Your vision.

They have hands but cannot feel. We have been rendered impotent and useless to do anything with human hands. Without Your Spirit, we are helpless.

~~~~~
## "Make us goal-oriented in the Lord."
~~~~~

They have feet but cannot walk. We go nowhere except we are carried along by the Spirit of the Lord. Otherwise, all activity becomes an exercise in futility. For this, Lord, we repent and ask forgiveness (Psalm 115:4-8).

Forgive us, Lord, for getting involved in good things which You never called us to. We acknowledge the fact that the good is the enemy of the better and the better is the enemy of the best. Lord, we want Your best. We want to go for the gold. Help us to do as Paul stated in Philippians 3:13, 14.

". . .Forgetting what is behind and straining toward what is ahead, I press on toward the goal to win the prize for which God has called me heavenward in Christ Jesus."

Make us goal oriented in the Lord. Lord, help us to buy up the time and apply our hearts to wisdom. God forbid that we, like a chicken, peck around in the dirt, groveling in the things of this world, when You have a higher calling for us to ascend into a rarified stratosphere of the Spirit like eagles. Help us this day to be challenged and so moved that we, with great resolve, take the high road. From here on out, for the rest of our lives, we shall forsake flesh and pursue the Spirit of the Lord. Every day is going to count for eternity.

We forsake confidence in every other stronghold except You. We refuse the false refuge of humanism and the arm of flesh. We refuse to look to Pharaoh's worldly protection or Egypt's shade for refuge. For Pharaoh's protection will be our shame and Egypt's shade will bring us disgrace. We acknowledge Lord, that

"No king is saved by the size of his army; no warrior escapes by his great strength. A horse is a vain hope for deliverance; despite all its great strength it cannot save."

Psalm 33:16, 17

Our confidence for safety, protection, watch care and welfare is in You. You are our strong defense in the day of battle. Thank You for hearing our prayer.

In Jesus' name we pray. Amen.

~ 24 ~

MARRIAGES

 timestamp timestamp timestamp

Dear Lord, we pray Your life into homes in this city. You have given us the ministry of reconciliation. Through prayer we exercise it on behalf of marriages. Let Your light shine so bright and the awesome life of the Lord Jesus be so evident in our homes that it would dispel darkness, oppression, strife, deception, separation, and in the place of this bring compassion, passion, forbearance and harmony. Lord, it's where the brethren dwell together in unity that You command a blessing. Let conditions be such in our home and marriages that You would see fit to command a blessing on us and our children (Psalm 133:1, 2).

Lord, we stand in the gap for marriages that are hanging by a thread. For the sake of husbands and wives, for the sake of our children and homes, for the sake of the Body of Christ, rend the heavens and come down. Salvage these homes. Put them back together and heal marriages in this city. Through intercessory prayer we exercise the ministry You have entrusted to us--the ministry of reconciliation.

Lord, Your Word says in Isaiah 1:18,

"Come now, let us reason together,. . . though your sins are like scarlet they shall be white as snow;. . ."

~~~~~

"We pray that You would purge from us schizophrenia so that those around us will not be nervous, not knowing which personality they are dealing with at the moment."

~~~~~

We pray that wives and husbands would be willing to reason together. We stand against those elements which prevent couples from reasoning together. We know the adversary, the devil, prowls around like a roaring lion looking for marriages to devour. Our enemy is unreasonable. Spirits of separation, division and divorce are unreasonable. We pray for marriages which are hanging in the balance, that husbands and wives would be willing to reason together and allow the Lord to pour in the oil of His Spirit to bring healing.

We intercede for marriages which have lost their first love. By Your grace, help us, instead of vexing, aggravating, accusing, provoking, angering, and stirring up the worst in each other, help us to draw out the best in each other. Restore the first love in our homes. Cast out the raging bull which tramples our families. Breathe on our families and marriages with a fresh breath of God. Restore the sound of rejoicing in our tents.

Just as You chose a wedding to perform Your first miracle and turned something bland into something pungent and powerful, and just as You transformed water into wine, so we ask You just as miraculously to breathe a fresh breath into marriages in this city, and turn that which is bland like water into the powerful new wine of Your Spirit. Come, Lord Jesus. Rend the heavens and come down. Visit Your people in this city this day.

Lord, give us single vision. Forgive us for being double-minded. Forgive us and heal us from having more than one distinct personality. We pray that You would purge from us schizophrenia so that those around us will not be nervous, not knowing which personality they are dealing with at the moment. Lord, You make people whole. You make them one. Make us whole. Make us one. Help us to have a single mind for You and a single eye for our spouses. Let not our eyes or mind wander. Help us to nip situations in the bud before they germinate, take root, and grow into a serious problem.

We pray that every man listening would be up-to-date with his God and up-to-date with his wife and keep short accounts so that his prayers will not be hindered. We pray that instead of husbands and wives trying to change each other, they would take hands off, pray diligently, and witness You going to the basement of their lives bringing about radical, pivotal changes of personality and lifestyle. You promised that those who called upon You would be delivered. Let not demon spirits be the spoiler in our lives or homes. Rid them from our marriages, from our children, from our finances. Reverse the curses, including generational ones, and bring such a radical metamorphosis in our lives, and deal so resolutely with spirits of deprivation, that we would begin to tear down our barns and build bigger just to contain the inordinate blessings of the Lord.

We pray that the light of Your Word and the brilliance of Your Spirit would expose every treacherous, devious, cunning, crafty work of darkness which gnaws at and undermines the unity in marriage. We corporately, as a body of prayer warriors, expose and take a resolute stand against spirits of separation, division, divorce, infidelity; those spirits which carefully set up and sponsor affairs; spirits of fornication, adultery, pornography and spirits of deception. We ask You, Lord, to deal with evil influences which encroach on marriages to cause eyes to be turned, attention to be diverted, and removes our focus from You and our spouses.

In the place of all of these works of darkness, we pray into our marriages a new zest, new life, the fire of the Lord, enthusiasm, joy, intimacy, tenderness, care, forbearance, patience, breathing room, liberty and vision. Let the love of God be manifest in our lives for our spouses and our family. Help us, like You, Lord, to be willing to lay down our lives for one another.

In Jesus' name we pray. Amen.

~ 25 ~

REPENTANCE

❧

Dear Lord, we acknowledge that every historic spiritual awakening was preceded by humility, repentance, forgiveness and heart-rending prayer that got Your attention, rent the heavens and caused You to come down. We confess Your Word that says,

"If my people, who are called by my name, will humble themselves and pray and seek my face and turn from their wicked ways, then will I hear from heaven and will forgive their sin and will heal their land."

2 Chronicles 7:14

Your Word also says that when we repent, and turn to You, our sins will be wiped out and times of refreshing will come from the Lord. Many of Your people are crying out to You from a barren, parched, desolate, sun-baked, weary land. Some are languishing in a state of fatigue, weariness, dissipation of energies, exhaustion and are on the threshold of burnout. They need a season of refreshing. We hold up those whose bodies are racked with pain, having suffered from spirits of infirmity, maladies, chronic illnesses and are candidates for the showers of refreshing upon their physical bodies.

We are candidates of the refreshing wind of the Holy Spirit to once again blow through our lives. Re-invigorate us with resurrection vitality. We claim Your Word that says, if we confess our sins you are faithful and just to forgive us our sins and cleanse us from all unrighteousness (1 John 1:9).

We thank You, Lord, You are not only our Redeemer, but You work so redemptively in our lives. You are the One Who restores the years where the cankerworm, caterpillar, locust worm and palmer worm have eaten (Joel 2:25). You do all things well.

We ask You to search our hearts. See if there be any wicked way. We can't afford to have this prayer short-circuited. Help us to come and reason with You that though our sins **". . . are like scarlet, they shall be as white as snow; though they are red as crimson, they shall be like wool" (Isaiah 1:18).**

Thank You for cleansing us of all our resentment, bitterness, anger, presumptuous sins and hidden faults. We confess to You all of our shortcomings, ulterior motives and hidden agendas. Help us, Lord, to be real people. We don't have to operate under a cloud of foreboding darkness with unsettled issues.

Let the way be clear; let nothing stand in the way. We pray that we will be up-to-date with You and each other. By the grace of God, let Your people keep short accounts. Let it not be said of any that they were turned over to the tormentors because they were forgiven so much and didn't, in comparison, forgive so little (Matthew 18:34, 35). We acknowledge that we cannot afford the luxury of harboring resentment, bitterness, unforgiveness, and right now, we mentally tear up all of our IOU's. We choose to forgive everyone who has ever hurt us.

Let not the root of bitterness, spoken of in scripture, spring up.

"See to it that no one misses the grace of God and that no bitter root grows up to cause trouble and defile many."

Hebrews 12:15

Just like John the Baptist prepared the way of the Lord, so we, right now, prepare the way for the Lord to come foursquare upon Christians in this area.

We thank You for Your Word that says,

". . .if we walk in the light, as he is in the light, we have fellowship with one another, and the blood of Jesus, his Son, purifies us from all sin."

1 John 1:7

Before this prayer is over, let no one who is participating feel yucky, dirty, oppressed, or unforgiven. Help them to realize as they just turn and repent, ask forgiveness, and are cleansed by the precious Blood of Jesus Christ, that they are totally forgiven, totally clean and their sins are cast as far as the east is from the west. There is no east pole, no west pole. There is no way of locating them. Their sins are cast into the deepest sea, never to be retrieved again. Help them to know of a surety, that as they repent and turn to You and receive Your Son, Jesus Christ, as their Personal Savior, they are in Christ's righteousness and justified--just as if they had never sinned (Psalm 19:13).

Forgive us for even momentarily agreeing with and strengthening satan's hand or being one of his supporters by being used as an accuser of the brethren. Lord, for this we repent and ask Your forgiveness and cleansing by the precious Blood of Jesus. We thank You that You promised us in Isaiah 58, if we would meet Your simple conditions, fast and pray, and cease the pointing of the finger, criticizing and accusing one another, incredible things would begin to burst forth in our lives.

By the grace of the living God, we will meet the conditions in Isaiah 58 and become recipients of these blessings.

"The Lord will guide you always; he will satisfy your needs in a sun-scorched land and will strengthen your frame. You will be like a well-watered garden, like a spring whose waters never fail. Your people will rebuild the ancient ruins and will raise up the age-old foundations; you will be called Repairer of Broken Walls, Restorer of Streets with Dwellings."

Isaiah 58:11, 12

Just like soldiers marching along and all of a sudden do an about face, 180 degrees, so we repent. We turn from our own righteousness, independence and idolatry. We turn away from the arm of flesh and the genius of humanism. We turn from our own ways, from indulgence in darkness, from dabbling in this world system, from looking to the bankrupt and leaking cisterns of our society and from our own answers. We fully turn to You and throw the entire weight of our lives, personalities, families, marriages, welfare, future and everything we have and are, on to You.

We repent of allowing the enemy to overrun our walls, sneak into our homes and take our children captive while we are asleep. We repent on behalf of the Church of America that in the last Presidential election *[1996]*, nearly fifty percent of registered Christians didn't even trouble themselves enough to vote. Help them to realize what You say in Psalm 12:8.

"The wicked freely strut about when what is vile is honored among men."

We repent of our lethargy which has allowed the same conditions to prevail as in Isaiah's day which produced a dearth of heroes, warriors, judges, prophets, elders, captains, men of rank, counselors and skilled craftsmen (Isaiah 3:1-3). Lord, bring back to America Godly statesmanship.

We repent for having made peace with mediocrity, for lapsing into a slough of despondency and self-pity, for allowing life to become routine and stale, and for falling into a rut. By the grace of God, it's going to be different. We're going to take the high road. Lord, Your people need some Divine CPR. Let this not be just another ordinary religious, perfunctory prayer. Breathe an anointed fresh breath of God upon those who are participating, so much so that they'll drop their anchor and with great decisiveness, look back on this day and say, "I have never been quite the same."

On behalf of the Church of the Lord Jesus Christ, we repent of not seeking You with our whole heart, mind and strength. We repent of allowing our spiritual muscles to atrophy. We repent of lapsing into a spiritually vegetative state while a battle rages over our head. Forgive us for our naivete and ignorance of the spiritual warfare which is ravaging the Church.

We repent, Lord, of our apathetic attitude. Lift us off our laps of luxury, our desire to gratify the flesh with inordinate self-aggrandizement. We repent of the lust of the flesh, the lust of the eyes and the pride of life, our haughty attitudes and arrogant ways. Lord, forgive the Church in this city and America for breathing in the anesthesia of the spirit of this age, lapsing into a state of spiritual stupor and being mesmerized by anemic religion. Forgive us, Lord, for the Church resembling so much the world that the world cannot tell the difference. Forgive us, Lord, for losing the ability to blush (Jeremiah 3:3).

We confess prayerlessness, carnality and being a lover of pleasure more than lover of God. We repent of control and manipulation which is rampant in our society and the Church. Forgive us, Lord, for maneuvering, leveraging, fancy footwork, shadow-boxing, manipulating and controlling people and situations through the most subtle of means which in its essence is witchcraft. Deliver us from being so insecure that

~~~~~

"Help us, Lord, instead of vexing and stirring up wrath in each other, to provoke one another to love and good deeds (Hebrews 10:24)."

~~~~~

we feel we need to compensate for feelings of inferiority by controlling others. We also repent of possessiveness, dominance and jerking people around.

We acknowledge and humbly confess, Lord, that because of the ravages of sin, involvement in this world system, being exposed to a pornographic society, fighting to make a livelihood, grasping for more and more, drinking at the cesspools of this secular system, that this has caused our hearts to become hard, our consciences cauterized, our compassion has calloused, our sensitivities seared as with a hot iron, and for this we repent and ask forgiveness. Lord, do a number on our hearts. Break up the fallow ground. We invite You to do as it says in Ezekiel 11:19.

"I will give them an undivided heart and put a new spirit in them; I will remove from them their heart of stone and give them a heart of flesh."

We confess, Lord, that we have been caught up in the whirlwind, hectic, fast-paced, jet-set, pressurized rush of our frenzied society and have neglected some of the more important things in life, run roughshod over our loved ones and people that really matter to us and for this we repent and ask forgiveness.

116

To whatever extent the ether waves of the spirit of this age have caused us to lapse into a desensitized, perfunctory, automated, cold, calculating zombie-like state where we are rude, unfeeling, harsh, unloving, and unable to empathize or feel someone else's pain, we humbly repent and ask forgiveness. Help us, Lord, instead of vexing and stirring up wrath in each other, to provoke one another to love and good deeds (Hebrews 10:24). To be sure we have covered everything, we repent of:

- **Bitterness, resentment, hatred, unforgiveness, violence, temper, anger, retaliation, murder** *[We tear up mental IOU's and since You said vengeance is Mine, I will repay, we release vengeance from our lives.]*

- **Retaliation, destruction, spite, hatred, sadism, hurt and cruelty**

- **Accusation, judging, criticism and faultfinding**

- **Lust, fantasy lust, homosexuality, lesbianism, adultery, fornication, harlotry and indulging in pornography** *[We thank You, Lord, that though our sins be as scarlet, You can make us as white as snow (Isaiah 1:18). Renew our minds by the washing of the Word.]*

- **Rebellion, self-will, stubbornness, disobedience, anti-submissiveness and incorrigibility** *[Since rebellion is as the sin of witchcraft, we repent of that also.]*

- **Strife, contention, bickering, argument, quarreling and fighting**

- **Entertaining rejection, fear of rejection and self rejection** *[Thank You, Lord, that we are accepted in the Beloved. We* *are the apple of Your eye and precious in Your sight. Help us by Your grace to be released from rejection.]*

- **Depression, despair, despondency, discouragement, defeatism, dejection, hopelessness, gloom, heaviness, suicide and death** *[We celebrate Your Word which states we can exchange the spirit of despair for the garment of praise and ashes for beauty (Isaiah 61:3). Since we have a choice between life and death--we choose life.]*

Thank You, Lord, for Your mercy, that when we forgive and ask forgiveness from You that You sweep our "**. . .offenses like a cloud,. . . our . . .sins like the morning mist" (Isaiah 44:22).**

"Let the wicked forsake his way and the evil man his thoughts. Let him turn to the Lord, and he will have mercy on him, and to our God, for he will freely pardon."

Isaiah 55:7

"For I will forgive their wickedness and will remember their sins no more."

Hebrews 8:12

In the name of Jesus we pray. Amen.

DAVID L. THOMAS
(1939-2000)

David L. Thomas was an ordained minister and co-founder of *Intercessors International, Inc.* With over 30 years in ministry, he served in many capacities, some of which were—interim pastor, missionary, corporate and hospital chaplain, television and radio speaker, board member of several ministries, guest speaker at churches, conferences and seminars around the country, and on numerous occasions, led the National Day of Prayer from the square in Marietta, GA as well as from the capitol steps in Atlanta, GA. Prayer was his belief and passion with a strong desire to see the House of God turned back into a House of Prayer for all nations.

INTERCESSORS INTERNATIONAL, INC.
P. O. Box 450093
Atlanta, GA 31145
(404) 330-1906

Intercessors International, Inc. is a 501(c)(3), non-profit ministry founded by David and Lynn Thomas as an international, non-denominational, full gospel intercessory prayer ministry to network, instruct, challenge, encourage and call forth intercessors in preparation for the last day harvest and spiritual awakening. One of their primary burdens is to see the modern American Church reduced back to the simplicity which is in Christ Jesus (2 Corinthians 11:3), and returned back to its initial mandate to be known as a House of Prayer for all nations (Mark 11:17). This is accomplished by a "Jeremiah Prayer Anointing" which uproots, tears down, destroys and overthrows man's humanistic religion so the Lord can build and plant His true New Testament Church (Jeremiah 1:10). They strongly believe in Paul's admonition, "the kingdom of God is not a matter of talk, but of power" (1 Corinthians 4:20).

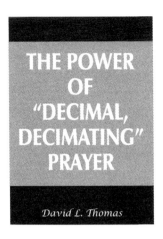

THE POWER OF
"DECIMAL, DECIMATING"
PRAYER

5-3/8 x 8-1/4   112 pages
Quality Paperback
ISBN# 0-9718249-3-2

This book details the power and importance of corporate prayer. When believers come together to pray, their prayers have the potential to change any situation, no matter how big or how small. Titles include:

♦   *One of Satan's Main Tactics*
♦   *The Amazing Power of Just One Person's Prayers*
♦   *Why You Have Been So Resisted*
♦   *Prayer Exposes the Enemy*

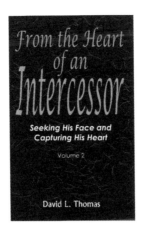

FROM THE HEART OF AN INTERCESSOR
VOLUME 2
Seeking His Face and Capturing His Heart
5-3/8 x 8-1/4   183 pages
Quality Paperback
ISBN# 0-9718249-4-0

This book contains a collection of intercessory prayers that provide
encouragement, hope, comfort, and stamina to stand in hard places. Prayer
is the "John the Baptist" of our day—it prepares the way of the Lord. In
David L. Thomas' own words:

*"We're about to witness the most incredible, magnetic drawing power of the
Holy Spirit known to mankind. The Church is beginning to flow in sync
with the Spirit. . . .When the Church is in agreement with and flowing
together with the Spirit in intercessory prayer, the amazing result is an
invitation which will impact all mankind and reverberate through the corridors
of this nation. . . .It will literally arrest this whole nation and eventually be
the major topic of conversation everywhere. This is going to happen in your
lifetime. "*

To order additional copies of:

- *From The Heart of an Intercessor Volume 1*
- *The Power of "Decimal, Decimating" Prayer,*
    or
- *From The Heart of an Intercessor Volume 2*, contact:

Anderson Publishing
P. O. Box 5544
Douglasville, GA 30154

e-mail address:
canderson@andersonpub.com

website address:
www.andersonpub.com